STAYING HUMBLE

The Journey of Building a High-Performance Team

By: Patrick J. Hall

Printed in the United States of America

STAYING HUMBLE: The Journey of Building a High- Performance Team — *1st Edition*

ISBN: 978-1-953610-47-8

1. Title
2. Business Management
        Human Resources & Personnel Management
        Business Decision Making
        Workplace Culture
3. Leadership & Motivation
4. Management Science

Cover design by Alishba Shah

NFB
NFB Publishing/Amelia Press
119 Dorchester Road
Buffalo, New York 14213
For more information please visit
nfbpublishing.com

"A leader is a rare person who comes along, raises the standards of excellence, captures the hearts of many, and inspires a group of individuals to achieve the impossible."

~Michael Jordan

Dedication

This book is dedicated to God for providing me the opportunities in life, my family for all the support they have provided to me, my leadership mentors throughout my career, and the Eagles team members I had the privilege of leading.

TABLE OF CONTENTS

Why I Wrote the Book

I WROTE THIS BOOK for three reasons: document a portion of my life for my kids and grandchildren to read, help people translate some great leadership lessons into actionable ways to build a high-performing team, and celebrate the journey of the Eagles team members who put their trust in me during my time with them.

When I was 26 years old, I prepared for my first combat deployment and my newly wedded wife handed me a blank journal and said, "I always remember my grandpa telling me he wished he would have documented his time during WWII, so his kids and grandchildren could read about different parts of his life. I started the first journal entry for you, and it would be great if you could document what you want and feel is right to talk about." I left a few days later for Kandahar, Afghanistan and spent the next year writing about the friendships I made, the missions I flew, the good times, bad times, the rest and recovery (R&R) with my wife in New Zealand, emotions I was feeling at the time, and leadership lessons I observed or experienced. I wrote in another journal for my second deployment and captured similar elements of my life at the time.

As I prepared to transition out of the military, I discovered I had been given leadership opportunities many people never get to experience, and that I had a unique ability to influence people in a positive way through the lessons I learned. To effectively transition my military skills into the business world, I read a lot of books by amazing authors about leadership, business, team building, and strategy. I discovered I do not have a great memory, and when I read a book, I do not retain the knowledge very well. I picked up another empty journal and began writing down all the key takeaways from each book that would help me in my leadership and business journey. This quickly became the one tool I went to on a daily basis to revisit the leadership lessons I had learned and read.

As I joined my first company, I had a long commute and learned about podcasts, so I began listening to leadership and business shows. I documented the lessons and great ideas I heard in my journal. Particular situations would occur at work that felt relevant to the things I was reading and listening to, so I used my new business team as a "testing ground" for the theories and lessons learned. Over time, I figured out what worked and what did not. I began to develop a playbook on how to build a team regardless of the performance state they currently were in. As I moved from team to team, company to company, I fine-tuned that playbook and it is now worth sharing with others.

Many credible authors I have read over the years started their own companies, were CEOs, held high ranks in the military, or had PhDs in leadership. Most of the readers of these books are professionals just starting out in a first-time leadership role with direct reports, having a challenging moment with their teams, or are leaders passionate about learning different techniques from other people. Sometimes it is hard for readers to relate to these authors or put themselves in the shoes of people who have so much "star power" or to even believe they can use the book to do the same things the author speaks of. Not all elements of the leadership books I read in the past worked for all situations. Not all books were great or applied to what I was experiencing. In contrast, I think the majority of readers will find my story very relatable and will be able to picture themselves in the scenarios I discuss in the book. It is based upon the story of an operational team, but the tools can be applied to any business career field. I did not reinvent ideas; I took the different lessons from the hundreds of leadership books I read, podcasts I listened to, seminars I attended, and great mentors I had throughout my life, put them into my toolkit, created my own brand of leadership, and leveraged the principles to develop high performing teams I had the privilege of leading.

My story shows step by step how to build a sustainable high-performing team by walking through the transformation of a particular team I led, The Eagles. This was not the first or the last team I led, but it was a three-year portion of my life where I truly implemented all the areas of team building and leadership I learned throughout my career up to the point I joined that team. There are team members who were with me throughout the whole journey, some who left during it, and some who are still carrying the torch today. They deserve to be celebrated and for other people to hear about their story and journey to greatness.

INTRODUCTION

I AM A "MILLENNIAL." Many employers complain that millennials are cocky, entitled, lazy, impatient, headstrong and do not listen to what anyone else has to say.[1] For me, nothing could be further from the truth. Some of what I include in this book I learned in person or from books written by past CEOs—either from their successes or their mistakes. However, most of it came by working hard and learning from my own experiences—positive AND negative.

Anyone who writes a book must satisfactorily answer one or two questions; for example, "Why would anyone want to read this book?" or "Why should they listen to me?"

The answer, I believe, is because I have taken a leadership approach over the course of my career that comprises theories and practices from a wide range of iconic leaders like leadership author and pastor John Maxwell, team dynamics expert Patrick Lencioni, and British inspirational speaker Simon Sinek, as well as president Abraham Lincoln, basketball coach John Wooden, and football coach Nick Saban. Their examples have helped me to build successful teams of all sizes within the operations and supply chain industries. The hardest parts of being a leader are influencing people and finding and bringing together individuals from different backgrounds who can deliver the most positive results. That might seem like an easy thing to do, but I can assure you it is not, which is why companies spend a lot of money employing leaders with these qualities.

Behavioral scientist and best-selling author, Steve Maraboli, said: "I don't want my life to be defined by what is etched on a tombstone. I want it to be defined by what is etched in the lives and hearts of those I've touched." Whether you are a new leader developing a team of two or an experienced leader developing a team of 1,000, the formula for success remains the same, and the principles discussed in this book will help you to develop and hone your skills to become a better leader. People are more likely to follow a leader who a) has a vision of how to make a difference in the world and b) has a positive influence on the people he/she leads. If you only care about your own success over that of the team, then you should not be in a leadership position. Why? Because leadership is not a top-down position, it is a position of service. You have an awesome responsibility—a responsibility not only to the employees and team members you serve, but also to the families of those you serve. Do not take that duty lightly.

You should read this because the focus of this book is building a team committed to the parallel visions of service and of making a difference. Many books about leadership and team-building talk in generalities, but I offer a concrete plan with examples that you can follow in order to achieve results. Although no two teams develop in exactly the same way, you CAN create a team where each member is striving for the vision while accepting 100% ownership of the results by employing the traits presented in this book.

CHAPTER ONE:

THE ROOTS OF LEADERSHIP

"I'm no self-made man...I am who I am because of those who
cared enough about me to touch my soul."

~ Mark Tabb

ON SEPTEMBER 11, 2001, the world changed with the collapse of the twin
towers. I, like everyone, remember what I was doing when I saw the horror
on the television screen. I was 18 years old and did not know how it would
impact my life in Michigan. As days, weeks, months, and years passed,
the country attempted to get back to normal. On September 11, 2011 the
9/11 museum and memorial opened to commemorate the attacks.[1] On
November 3, 2014 One World Trade Center opened.[2] After the twin towers crumbled, there was so much concrete from the wreckage that it took
10 years to build a memorial and 13 years to construct another building.
Imagine if the builders started the One World Trade Center Tower and the
9/11 Memorial Museum on top of the rubbage. It would not be a smooth
foundation to build from. Instead, the builders and volunteers spent many
years clearing out the concrete from the tragedy, and then figured out what
would be built in its place to honor the heroes and victims. Building a team
is no different; there must be a smooth base and foundation to build from.
Some team structures may be so broken they need to start from scratch

and make sure anything left over from the old structure is removed. Other teams may have a good, solid foundation, but are a little old, rusty, and in need of some polishing. The purpose of this book is to help you become a better leader and team builder regardless of the initial shape of your foundation.

MY FIRST TASTE OF LEADERSHIP: STRENGTH & HONOR IN HIGH SCHOOL
I grew up in Southwest Michigan in a middle-class family. I am the youngest of three boys and have loving and caring parents. Both of my brothers played sports and were passionately competitive. They set the bar high! By the time I entered high school I was already very driven and had set lofty goals for myself. I wanted to play varsity football as a freshman. I wanted to play five sports in a year. And I wanted to graduate number one in my class academically.

As my eighth-grade year ended, I immediately began strenuous workouts. In fact, I worked out three times a day. I made a sign that read STRENGTH & HONOR. Russel Crowe said this phrase in Gladiator, and I connected to the ruggedness of it. If I were to achieve my goals, I was going to need to be tough, disciplined, and rugged. I woke up at 5:00 in the morning every day to go to the YMCA to lift weights, and I followed a strict regimen of focusing on one muscle group at a time during the workout. After the gym, I would run the sand dunes, swim, run the stadium stairs, do sprints on the track, or bike (I am sure I learned everything from Rocky IV where Rocky trains to fight Ivan Drago). Next, I would go back to the YMCA to conduct another round of weight lifting. I did this from June to August to get ready for football.

Coaches and future teammates gradually heard about my workout routine. I invited others to work out with me, and I led them through the sessions. This was my first real taste of leadership and influencing others around me regardless of age, experience, or athletic ability. I set the tone for the day, the expectation for the workout, and the desired results I wanted to see. By the time "High School Football Hell Week" started, we were in far better shape in mind and body than the other football players.

FIRST OBSTACLE: SPORTS

When the season started, I was placed on the junior varsity football team. However, the day before our first game, I tore my MCL. I had never experienced such pain in my whole life, and I was bitter. I felt that three months of training had gone down the drain. Back then, an MCL tear was an eight-week (minimum) recovery period with a lot of rehabilitation. I remembered that Vince Lombardi said, "The harder you work, the harder it is to surrender." I decided to add one more goal to my lengthy list—to recover and be ready to play football again within four weeks–half the prescribed time. I woke up early every day prior to class to rehab my knee and followed my trainer's guidance. I achieved this goal, and after four weeks I was back on the field wearing a bulky brace.

The varsity team made the playoffs that year and the coach invited me to come practice with them. I worked my tail off and I ended up on the kickoff recovery team. At the start of the playoff game, I made the first tackle on the kickoff. That tackle, although remembered only by me and my parents, was the greatest sense of accomplishment a 15-year-old boy could have. It was proof to me that if I worked hard enough, I could control my own destiny.

As football season ended, the varsity wrestling coach asked me to join the team instead of playing basketball. I was torn because basketball was a team sport and I loved both sports. At five feet, nine inches, I knew I was never going to be a collegiate wrestler or a great basketball player, but I felt I added value to both teams. The wrestling coach said it would be okay if I played both basketball and wrestling, so I talked to the basketball coach. He was ok with it as long as when there was a conflict I went with basketball, since it was a team sport. I had bitten off a lot to chew!

My day was pretty brutal. I would wake up at 7:00 a.m., go to school and then to wrestling practice from 3:00-5:00 p.m. Basketball practice followed for two more hours. And if that wasn't enough, I began dating my high school sweetheart Katherine (who is now my wife), and I would try to spend time with her in the evening. That meant I started my homework at

11:00 p.m. or midnight in the basement. I turned our ping-pong table into a desk. Not sure why, but I think I remember my dad doing his work down there, and then my brother did it as well, so I followed suit.

Wrestling got interesting because I made the varsity team as a freshman, which put more pressure on the situation because I had to choose the freshman basketball team over a varsity wrestling match when there was a conflict per my agreement with the basketball coach. This created some friction with the seniors on the team, who were not happy with my decisions. However, I stayed mission-focused knowing this was what I had to do to play five sports in the year. I remember vividly to this day a wrestling match I was winning until I made a mistake which placed me on my back, and I got pinned by my opponent, causing six points to go to the other team. My wrestling coach reminded me for 15 minutes about how I never would have made that mistake if I had been more focused on wrestling, and to just give up on basketball. He made it really personal. From this, I learned that there are only so many hours in a day and that pleasing everyone is impossible, so it is important to make sure that my intentions are clear with regard to the team. This does not necessarily mean absolute buy-in, but it does mean there should be absolute clarity between my role and that of my teammates.

The sport I really loved but did not have access to at the high school level was hockey, so I joined an adult league that played on Sunday nights. I drove with my goalie friend Jeff (in his mid-40s) 45 minutes to play our games. This was my first opportunity to lead teammates who were much older than me, an experience which ended up playing a huge role in my professional career. I was 15 years old playing with 30- to 45-year-old men, some of whom had kids my age.

This was intimidating at first; however, I learned that each person, regardless of age, plays an important role on the team. Because I was active in other sports, I was quick, nimble, and had more endurance than my teammates. This advantage allowed me to help my teammates out when they became tired earlier than I did. On the flip side, I respected their knowledge of the game; they understood strategy and how the game should be played. I asked a lot of questions, and they were eager to help me learn. I was able to use motivational tactics to rally our teammates to many wins. I soon realized that none of them looked at me as a kid; they relied on me as a teammate.

I came out of that basketball and wrestling season a better person and had a small break before I had to make another tough decision between track and baseball. Again, I talked to both coaches and each agreed to let me play both sports as long as I played baseball (the team sport) when there was a conflict. My days were similar to those during wrestling and basketball. I went to baseball practice with my team after school, and then my track coach would tell me the workout for the day; I performed the workout after baseball practice. My track coach stayed with me every once in a while, but it was mostly on me to finish the workout. I developed the discipline to conduct the workout even when no one checked on me, knowing that my teammates had endured the same training. My track team won the state championship that year, and I ran the first leg of the 4x100 relay in the State finals. To add even more to my plate, I played on a travel soccer team on Sundays.

Although the year had taken a toll on my body, I accomplished my goal of playing five high school sports while also playing two other sports on the side. I eventually became captain of four different sports teams, one while I was a junior. I maintained a 3.9 GPA throughout all four years. I ended up having an amazing high school sports experience and grew as a leader and person.

TAKING THE NEXT STEP: ADDING STRUCTURE

I had amazing teachers and coaches in high school who provided opportunities like the ones in my story where, if I was willing to put in the work, they were willing to take a chance on me. From them, I learned that leadership is about taking care of people. It does not matter what activities you involve yourself in or the background in which you come from, the Golden Rule is always in effect: Treat others as you would want to be treated. God gave me a gift of endurance and drive, and it would be on me if I wasted it.

I remember a Michael Jordan poster that stated, "A leader is a rare person who comes along, raises the standards of excellence, captures the hearts of many, and inspires a group of individuals to achieve the impossible." I set my goal and purpose to become that kind of leader.

Living a structured life makes things easier and more organized to achieve goals. I learned early on that setting goals for the day, week, season, year, and/or decade are what can set a good leader apart from others. I recently found a paper I wrote in high school that laid out specifically my goals for what I wanted to achieve in four years. It also had goals for individual football games, football seasons, academic goals, and financial goals. Goals are a tool to be used to keep your life on track. It is like using a sniper rifle to shoot a target 500 meters away; there might be wind that can cause the bullet to stray off course, but that can be corrected with minor adjustments. With no goals in place that are SMART (Specific, Measurable, Attainable, Realistic, with a Timeline),[3] it's like using a shotgun that can only hit a target that is big and close because you are hoping one of the little steel balls hits where you need it to. Hope is not a strategy.

WEST POINT: GOAL SETTING

My hard work and dedication in high school paid off, and I was hungry to learn more about leadership. Upon receiving an appointment from Representative Fred Upton, I decided to attend the United States Military Academy at West Point after high school. The events of September 11, 2001 occurred 10 months before my Plebe (freshman) year at West Point, and it was clear that the trials I endured during the past four years of high school were just the beginning, but they prepared me for what was to come.

I brought what I learned in high school into West Point. The United States Military Academy is a place that is beautiful, amazing, and has the ability to transform young adults. I am the leader I am today because of the lessons I learned at West Point. Other than the U.S. government, no company in the world can spend the amount of money on one individual to gain the leadership development that a cadet learns. Cadets learn structure, organization, and discipline. They first learn how to be a follower and then how to become a leader with character. They have the opportunity to make mistakes, fail, learn, and grow in a safe environment where there are no lives at stake. This is why Academy grads are so valuable in the business world today. They lead with influence, not rank on a collar. They lead from the front, not from behind. They put their teammates above themselves. They put the mission first above personal glory.

I had the honor to play on the Army sprint football team where I continued to grow as a person, teammate, and leader. Playing a Division I sport along with the academic rigors of the Academy instantly taught me how to prioritize and execute on the things that mattered. In my four years at West Point, I set weekly goals. The goals were specific and measurable for academic tests I had in class, how I wanted to perform in a football game, and what I wanted to accomplish in my social setting. Every Sunday, I graded myself with a plus or minus. I either met the standard set forth or I did not. Based on what I achieved, I gave myself anywhere from an A to an F for the overall week. There was always a picture below the goals with a leadership quote, and I taped it on my desk to look at every day. This is an organizational aspect that I see people not executing correctly. They make goals, but then forget about them because the goals are not sitting in front of them every day. Anyone can say they have a goal, but if it is written down and in front of you, then it becomes a kind of contract you would be breaking if you make excuses as to why you did not accomplish it. It's a way to hold yourself accountable for the results of the goal. Think about all the New Year's resolutions people make that end after the first week.

THE ARMY: LEARNING AND LEADERSHIP OPPORTUNITIES

After four years at West Point, I graduated and chose to serve in the Aviation branch. I spent 18 months at Fort Rucker, Alabama, for flight school. Ultimately, I became a UH-60L Blackhawk Pilot and reported to my first duty station at Fort Bragg, North Carolina where I spent seven years. I served two combat tours in Afghanistan which were the highlights of my Army career. I was a Company Commander, Platoon Leader, and Operations Officer. I learned that in order to build a team, standards and disciplines through accountability determines mission success. These are heavy words that must be fully understood. While in the Army, I began to see that I was blessed with opportunities to become the best leader possible and I became a student of leadership. I began reading as many books on leadership as I could. I began developing my personal leadership brand and how I wanted to impact the lives of those I served. I had an opportunity to acquire knowledge that I wanted to impart to others.

In my first role as a Company Commander, the Army taught me that age does not determine leadership. I was a 23-year-old kid who had the daunting responsibility of leading 93 soldiers who just returned from a combat deployment. Nearly all the soldiers were older than me with more experience, but instead of dwelling on that, I leveraged the great soldiers around me to grow as a leader. I gained the respect of my soldiers because I showed I cared by never asking them to do something I was not willing to do myself. I asked for their viewpoints on important decisions I had to make. Not all young officers were provided this unique opportunity, so I wanted to make the best of it.

As an aviator leading and flying missions in a combat environment, I learned to remain calm under pressure, manage a heavy task list, and put life into perspective. Most of the 250+ combat flights flown in Afghanistan involved planning high profile missions in which soldiers placed their lives in the hands of my crew and me. Whether I was on the flight controls or conducting navigation duties, I managed five radios and coordinated with attack helicopters, ground force units, headquarters, and air space controllers to make sure the correct decisions were made. Every time I went on a mission, there was a chance something could go wrong and I would not make it back alive. I was fortunate to make it home safely with lessons to leverage for the rest of my life.

BUSINESS CAREER: TRANSITIONING FROM LOW TO HIGH-PERFORMING
Upon fulfilling my commitment to the Army, I began working with Cameron-Brooks, a military recruiting firm for Junior Military Officers (JMOs)

getting out of the military to bridge the gap between what I did in the Army and adding value to a company in the business world. I interviewed with 13 companies in two days and a supply chain company called me to see if I would be interested in a distribution center in Georgia. I flew to Georgia to interview with the Vice President of the region. He let me know that the building was one of the best in the company and offered me a position to join the team. I told him I wanted to be a part of the worst team in the company, not the best. I believed the worst needed my leadership experience the most. He told me of a team in the eastern part of the state that was in need of a lot of help. I ended up taking over for the worst-performing team in the worst-performing distribution center in the company; a team of 100 team members and four Area Leaders.

I did not know much about distribution centers (DC), but I did have the skills I learned throughout my life to this point to influence a group of people to achieve great things. I spent the first 16 months of my business career on a second shift perishable grocery shipping and receiving team. I led the team from 'worst performing' into the top ten within seven months of joining the company. I did this by leveraging a combination of the leadership tactics that worked in the military, advice from the books I read, and lessons from mentors. If a tactic did not work for a particular situation, then I adjusted and tried a different approach.

As a result of the quick turnaround performance of the team, I gained the attention of the same VP who hired me. He asked me to help a Regional DC in Southwest Georgia. Ironically, this was the same DC that he had touted to me as being the best in the company. He asked me to come help for a few weeks as a consultant. After two weeks, I told him I would need to be part of the team in order to impact change. Within three months of joining the team, the culture began to shift in a positive way, and the performance began to improve. After nine months, the whole DC of 900 employees in a 1.5 million square foot building improved significantly in safety, performance, quality, and hourly team member engagement.

That same VP recommended me to a peer of his in Florida who was looking for someone to lead a whole DC team through a cultural and performance transformation. Through the different leadership challenges at the two DCs, I fine-tuned my operational knowledge, improved upon my team-building process, and used the momentum from each team to help improve the next.

I served the team members at this company for six years where I specialized in turning around poorly performing teams with poor cultures, bad performance, unsafe behaviors, and no personal or professional development of others.

This Florida DC is where our journey begins. I am going to show how I leveraged my past experiences in leadership to turn around a large operation within three years. With the help of some amazing leaders and teammates, I developed a Playbook for success and drove a vision to accomplish goals while instilling 100% ownership at all levels. In the next chapter, I will tell the story of the last operational team (The Eagles) I led for this company and show how all the hard-earned knowledge to this point was put to use. I break down the key elements to use with different types of teams.

The distribution center (DC) was located in a little town in Florida. To give them some cohesion and a sense of camaraderie, I convinced the team to give themselves a name. After spending 12 years in a military setting, I developed a love for the bald eagle which represents freedom, vision, strength, courage, new chances, and doing good. And, they just look awesome! Hence, when I suggested that the team name themselves The Eagles, the group loved it and it stuck.

If the reader takes away one skillset from this book to put in his or her leadership toolkit, I will consider it a success. There are, of course, concepts and elements within this book that are from other leadership and self-help books. Some of the concepts might seem simple and obvious, but leaders in business do not practice them daily, which impacts the culture of teams. People often ask me, "Patrick, what is the best book I can read right now to become a better leader?" I always tell them to read Dale Carnegie's *How to Win Friends and Influence People*. When people read the Carnegie book, they say it is all common sense, to which I respond, "If it is so simple, then why do we not do it every day? Why do we not practice those simple skills?"

KEY TAKEAWAYS OF CHAPTER 1:

1. "A leader is a rare person who comes along, raises the standards of excellence, captures the hearts of many, and inspires a group of individuals to achieve the impossible." ~Michael Jordan

2. Regardless of the experience or current state of a team, there must be a solid foundation to build from.

3. You should provide absolute clarity to what your role is on a team and that of your teammates.

4. Living a structured and organized life makes achieving goals easier.

5. If you are going to take the time to make a goal, then write it down in a place you will see every day, and then commit to achieving it.

6. In order to build a team, standards and disciplines through accountability determines mission success.

CHAPTER TWO:

THE EAGLES

"Leadership is leaders inducing followers to act for certain goals that represent the values and motivations, the aspirations and expectations of both leader and followers. And the genius of leadership lies in the manner in which the leaders see and act on their own and their followers' values and motivations."

~ James MacGregor Burns

FIRST CHALLENGE: OPERATION INDEPENDENCE DAY

I WAS WITH A supply chain company for two years with little knowledge of how supply chains function within big distribution centers (DCs), and I significantly enhanced the performance and culture of two medium-sized teams. As I mentioned earlier, a Vice President in Florida asked me to lead a struggling DC. I felt I was ready, but I needed to convince my wife to move away from her family in Atlanta, Georgia, to Jacksonville, Florida, for this opportunity. In this chapter, I will explain the high-level path that I took to turn this team around. When I refer to the phrase "turn around," I am talking about a team that is not performing to their highest potential due to lack of leadership. I will start from the first meeting I had with the leaders on the team and end with the results they achieved through the journey. I will explain my observations and actions taken in a way I think you, as the reader, can relate to in your own career. In subsequent chapters, I will dive deep into the processes by which the results were achieved. Each chapter will end with a recap and key takeaways. I will reference key points I learned from the Academy, the Army, the deployments, and other leaders over the years.

The new team I would be leading in Florida was part of a high-volume grocery distribution center servicing over 200 stores in the market. They were also the only DC to service the Caribbean, which involved more complicated port operations. Upon arriving, my first course of action was to take some time to deep dive into the financial numbers and asked a lot of questions of leaders within the company who were not members of the new team. I got my mind prepared for the correct approach to take with this team. The first team I led at the company had great leaders; however, the hourly team member base needed a lot of help understanding the vision and their purpose. The second building I joined had amazing hourly team members, but the leaders needed help to understand their various roles. I wondered what the issue was with this team. Why was it last in all major categories: safety, performance, financial metrics through profit and loss (P&L), quality, and team member incentive? Other company leaders did not want to be sent to this building for some reason.

Based on what I saw in the other two DCs, I assumed that the structure and organization of the team were probably very poor. After observing the full operation for less than one day, I could tell that the leaders lacked the proper planning to deliver a successful peak (holiday) season. I joined the team in June, a few weeks prior to the 4th of July, which is the biggest holiday (in terms of volume) for a grocery building. First, I held an initial meeting with my 12 senior leaders. I explained to them my expectations, which were to develop a sound plan where the safety of our teammates was No. 1 and the execution of 100% quality service to our stores a very close second. We began to brainstorm what success would look like for this 4th of July peak season. Everything I read about leadership and learned over the years suggested that I should not come in "hot" and start giving orders and making changes. So, this was a delicate situation because this initial period would set the tone for the rest of the year, but I did not have time to develop trust and credibility the way I normally would. In the meeting with the team, I chose my words carefully, was very clear about the expectations, and gave a detailed description of the importance of the "why." I used my experience from the Army to write an operations order prior to the meeting. The document laid out the situation, mission, contingencies, reporting structure, maintenance plans, and what the execution would look like. It also delegated specific tasks to each of the leaders and their teams to provide ownership and accountability. In the meeting, I read the Operations Order aloud and called it Operation Independence Day.

After sharing the Operation Independence Day document, I asked the leaders for their input on typical volume, potential barriers, and thoughts on contingencies. Normally, the leaders would have provided their input prior to me briefing them, but this was the first time any of them had experienced this level of detailed planning. They gave great feedback and many of their suggestions were valuable, so they were added to the five-page document. From there, I instructed the senior leaders to brief all the mid-level leaders and team members on the plan. I said, "The goal and only acceptable result is: zero accidents, zero medicals, zero scheduled departures missed, and zero service issues. If you take care of your team, they will take care of you." My senior leaders had a clear plan, and they were prepped on how the building would operate in the future. They needed to see a win from this planning, and they did. They achieved the goal, and they saw the value of putting the safety of the team before performance, which was something they were not accustomed to prior to that time.

BUILDING TRUST & CREDIBILITY
I spent the first month diving into the details of the performance and financial numbers, walking the floor, writing notes, and developing a strategy that would turn this building into a finely tuned machine capable of

running itself. I ended up with six pages of typed notes on the areas of the business needing to change. My experience from previous situations and operational strategies, books I had read, and leaders with whom I had interacted gave me confidence that we could become a top-ranking division within the company.

When first joining a team, it is important to observe and ask a lot of questions of team members. The leader needs to let the conversations flow and understand that the days will be long because it is difficult to set a time frame for this magnitude of change. Imagine having a deep conversation with an operator on the floor who might be seeing a decision-making leader for the first time in his or her career. This can be intimidating, causing the operator to feel vulnerable and reluctant to speak up. Or, on the other hand, he or she could be excited and want to talk for hours. Now, imagine five minutes into the conversation, the new leader cutting it short because of a timed agenda. More harm would occur at that moment than if there had not been an engagement with the operator in the first place. This is why the early stages of developing a team are all about building trust and credibility. Often, team members only see the new leader as someone who will make changes and adjustments to the "way things used to be."

THE LITTLE THINGS: GETTING TO KNOW MY LEADERS

During the first couple of months, I decided to spend more time getting to know the leadership team and to save the hourly team members for later in the journey. I sat down with all 60 salaried leaders to ask them questions about their families and hobbies and to lay out my "Leadership Contract" (I will go into detail in a later Chapter). This leadership contract consisted of 10 elements or principles by which I intended to lead. This was a way for my team to hold me accountable. The contract had statements such as, "I am never going to ask you to do something I am not willing to do myself" (more examples are in the Appendix). This helped set the tone with my leaders: before I told them what I expected of THEM, they knew what to expect from ME.

It's one thing to know about your leaders' spouses and kids and their interests; it's another to keep asking about their personal lives throughout your time with them. That is what caring is all about. When one of my leaders told me something about his or her personal life, I documented it in my notebook and put it on my calendar to ask about it in the future. When I asked about it the next time we talked, it showed that I truly cared; rather than something I just checked off my list of things to do. Calling a team member on his/her birthday is an easy gesture that has a huge impact. Spend a little time in the beginning putting every birthday into your calendar with a reminder and the leader's phone number.

OBSERVATIONS OF THE TEAM: DO THE LITTLE THINGS RIGHT

During my evaluation of the team, I went to my boss, and explained that I believed it might take as many as five years to completely turn this team and culture around. I told her there were 15 years of bad habits and poor standards and disciplines to overcome. I thought the hourly team members were great and the leaders were some of the best I had seen; the team was bent, not broken. I told her that I planned to take the team through the Four Stages of Team Development[1] and I laid out most of the strategy for her. I anticipated there would be factors and challenges I did not know about yet, but assured her that, ultimately, if we stayed the course during the tough times, the team would be better for it.

I told my boss that my first goal was to build trust and credibility with the team, and then I would seek to establish a structural foundation under the company policy and procedure "umbrella." By umbrella, I meant the thousands of Standard Operating Procedures (SOPs) and processes that the company already had in place that were supposed to be followed in every distribution center (over 160). I believed other managers had tried to fix the culture in the past but had mistakenly tried to build a foundation without starting with the basic elements of the business. To get my point across, I used the analogy of a large city building collapsing. After a city building falls, there is so much concrete from the wreckage that it is impossible to put anything new there. Imagine if the builders started the replacement skyscraper on top of the rubbage. It would not be a smooth foundation to build from and would eventually fall. Instead, builders spend many months clearing out the concrete, and only then can they establish a smooth base to build from. For the DC to be successful, the team and I needed to put in the time to smooth out the team's foundation. This would ensure success in the future.

The team needed to focus on doing the little things right. As Dave Ramsey, author and radio show host, would say, "We need to be excellent in the ordinary."[2] We were not performing the basic functions properly. Each team within the building had its own interpretation of each company SOP based on personal experiences and years with the company. Teams did not communicate with one another and leaders made decisions to complete the day as quickly as possible regardless of the outcome. The simple tasks throughout the day were not completed. This somewhat random approach was getting in the way of the team's success. And if a team cannot do the little things correctly, it will never be able to sustain more advanced operations. A basketball team does not start by practicing the alley-oop, they start by practicing how to pass properly. I explained to my boss that I was going to write out a "Standard Operating Procedure that was customized to our DC and specific to parts of the process that were not being performed correctly by the team, but which still fell within the company umbrella. We were going to establish a standard for running our Distribution Center.

I believe no two teams are exactly the same, so I had to treat my team differently than others within the company. I told my boss we were going to use the Lean Six Sigma methodology, which is a continuous improvement program to improve safety, quality, and team performance. Lean Six Sigma is a common methodology within operational environments, but is applicable to all business fields. Most importantly, I explained that I was going to establish an expectation based on standards and disciplines to which everyone in the building would be held accountable. A "standard" is an expectation the company has set for its team members, and "discipline" is the ability to do it right, day in and day out, no matter how mundane it seems. When you do things according to standards (the right way to do something), it becomes automatic like doing push-ups and sit-ups correctly to maximize results, which is something engrained in me from my high school training days.

One thing I noticed in the early days of my journey was that whenever a small crisis occurred, the leaders started "shooting from the hip." They would make decisions and make things happen without communicating to anyone or adhere to the company protocols. They truly thought there were human lives on the line. This was an area that I needed to address quickly. For example, about two months into my assignment to our distribution center, a water pipe was hit by one of our forklift drivers. The water flooded the dock and shut down the operation, which, in a high-volume distribution center like ours, can have disastrous consequences. As soon as I was informed, I made sure the water was turned off, then told every senior and key leader to meet me in an open conference room.

I could see a bit of panic on each person's face, so I calmly asked everyone to sit down. I asked, "Were any team members hurt?" The answer was, "No." I wrote down the situation on a white board and asked what actions we needed to take to get us operational (back to normal work). I told them a short story from my days in the Army as a Blackhawk pilot flying missions in Afghanistan where decision-making time equated to potential loss in life. I asked if there were any bullets flying in the distribution center, and the answer was again, "No." We calmly developed a sound plan in 15 minutes. The leaders felt as though they were a part of the solution versus being told what to do. It was the first time that different cross-functional teams within the building came together to accomplish a task. This seems like a small thing, but it was a huge win because it was the beginning of building trust on the team. The conference room was soon being called the War Room for any situation that came up, and there were many, many situations in the following years requiring the use of this room.

BASICS OF THE BUSINESS: KNOW YOUR ROLE

One problem was that each leader operated independently and differently from the others. The Area Leaders, who were the frontline salary managers, did not understand what their jobs entailed and what a typical day should look like, which caused them to miss the little details. Days were lost in chaos and they were just trying to survive. They had become really good firefighters, but leaders in survival mode can be unpredictable because they cannot see past the immediate work. They do not have a long-term vision, which is critical. They needed to learn to see past one day, one month, one quarter, or one year. I decided to write a document which would eventually become the foundation for the future of the DC. The document was called the "Back-to-Basics Standard Operating Procedure." It walked the leaders at all levels through their days and explained what "meeting expectations" would look like. The Back-Basics (B2B) SOP was essential to establishing the foundation for the team forward. It provided clarity to show what the future should look like and had the ability to tap into emotions, resulting in influence.[3]

The B2B SOP explained the expectations of leaders when they came into work on the first day each week. It explained the physical checks that needed to occur, such as face-to-face meetings with the leader coming off the current shift to see what the building and operational situation was in real-time. This would determine the next actions and steps to be taken. The document explained which administrative duties to examine and keep in front of them. It explained the importance of "tactically planning" their day. It is crucial to plan what the day and week will look like. A football team does not go to the line of scrimmage without everyone on the team understanding whether it is a pass play, run play, or something else. Once the quarterback starts the play, the plan can change, but at least all 11 players know what to do, which gives them a fighting chance of moving the ball (business) forward.

The B2B SOP offered my leaders a simple Microsoft Excel sheet that helped them determine how much labor was required for the day to be most efficient. It laid out the details of what a leader should do before the operation began, during the operation, and after the operation. It explained what a leader and team member would be held accountable for and what that accountability looked like. Some might think that is a form of micro-management; however, every team member should want to know what parameters they must operate within. And most importantly, high achievers want to know that everyone is held to the same standards of excellence. This helps to determine whether or not a leader has the right players on the field in the correct positions, and also whether the playing field has been adequately leveled so that everyone knows what "right" looks like.[4]

Many transformational leaders implement a structure but wonder why the structure fails to stick as a way of operating. The most important aspects of a change in leadership and putting a structure into place is the "rollout process." I believe in this so much that I wrote an SOP on how to properly roll out a program, process, or expectation. You cannot just write an email to your leaders about the new plan and expect it to stick. You cannot just write an SOP and then email it to the leaders or the team. You might have read from many authors that it takes a minimum of 21 days on average to change a behavior, and even then, a leader has to execute the change delicately. After I wrote the B2B SOP, I talked to several leaders and team members about it and asked what they would change or add. Once I felt it was a fair and consistent document, I brought all of the leaders into a room and briefed it. I did not rush it; I allowed for questions to be asked. I gave them talking points and a way to inform the rest of the team. I explained to them that the accountability would not start until one month after the complete rollout. This was to ensure they fully grasped the document and my expectations. I spent the next month walking the floor and talking to everyone about the change coming to the team. My belief was that if I could not explain the "why" behind what we were rolling out, then we probably should not do it because it was not simple enough.

Remember, the team was changing 15 years of poor behaviors and incorrect processes that were not in line with the company expectations.

Within five months of starting to establish structure with the team, the performance on all levels began to improve significantly but not without some setbacks. Leaders and team members started to believe in themselves and the process; however, just as the team began to build momentum, a few team members wrote a negative letter to corporate headquarters about my approach to team building (I will go into more detail about this later in the book). As a result, the team took several steps backward in their progress as I worked through the concerns of the senior leadership team within the company. My approach to team building was different than what many in the company had ever experienced. In any team building there will be some level of pushback and hesitancy by the team members experiencing the change. Although my team took several steps backward, we came out stronger on the other side. The performance of the team declined rapidly once the structure was removed for a short time period, but provided confidence to the leaders and team members that the work they put into the process had a positive impact. Once the corporate team understood what the leaders and I were in the process of building, they supported the change and the team began to perform at the level they were at before the letter was written.

REASON OR EXCUSE: "WE HAVE ALWAYS DONE IT THAT WAY."

The most dangerous phrase in the English language is, "We have always done it that way," and many times that was the excuse for not accepting the B2B SOP. It was often a struggle for both experienced and young leaders to grasp a different way of looking at the business and believe in themselves. My job, as the leader, was to get other leaders to think differently and to operate at a new level. Many of my leaders thought the goals were set too high and were therefore unachievable. In order to get through this time period, I knew I had to use analogies and easy terms to explain to the leaders how much more capable they would be of achieving the goals if they would look at the business from a different angle than they had in the past. I shared with them a quote by Albert Einstein: "No problem can be solved from the same level of consciousness that created it. You have to rise above it."[5] I conferred with many of the leaders one-on-one in my office, on the operational floor, and in their own environments to help them understand, and I was intentional about highlighting their wins when they occurred. This gave them confidence and momentum which are very critical in the early phases of building a team.

Eventually, after seven months, the team gained confidence and began to see results. The number of safety-related injuries declined and the operational performance improved. The working days got shorter and the whole team seemed happier. They had shifted their mindsets to believe that anything was possible.

As we gained momentum, I gradually allowed the leaders to own the decision-making, the planning, the development of other teammates, and the future of the DC. All the Standard Operating Procedures were specifically written for and integrated to our DC, and these became our "Playbook." The leaders now understood the importance of the Playbook and the structure behind the team. Leaders from other DCs within the company began to ask how we achieved such positive results. This caused the leaders in the Eagles to recognize the importance of a vision and setting yearly goals. The senior leaders had become major players in the strategy of the building. As the Eagles hit their stride, the rest of the company network started to see the benefits of structure and one consistent way of operating. I was asked to help out other teams that were not meeting their performance potential. This just added more credibility to the team and what we had accomplished. One VP even asked me to implement our Playbook in other DCs in her division. Ironically, this same VP had earlier engineered my most humiliating setback (explained later in another chapter).

A little more than two years into the journey, the company hired a new Executive Vice President who based the company strategy to go after its biggest competitor on a book called *The Art of the Possible* by Daniel Jacobs. There were so many similarities to what I was teaching my leaders that many of them asked if I based our structure and plan off this book. This Executive VP immediately started to work on a Playbook that held the key to consistency for all distribution centers within the company to operate. He focused on leadership and challenging the status quo. He was preparing to go toe-to-toe with our biggest competitor in every way. He used to talk about how working for the company for 25 years did not guarantee tenure. This was not said in a threatening way. He simply meant that longevity is good and experience is good, but just because you reached a certain number of years, it does not give you the right to go on cruise control. The competition is relentless and if you do not stay ahead of them, you will cease to exist.

This gave the team members even more confidence, and they did not have to change their mindsets because they had already been on this journey for the past couple years. The leaders in the DC started to share the ownership at all levels within the team to include the hourly team members. Why should the team members executing the operation on a daily basis not have ownership in the results? Gradually, I felt comfortable relinquishing control and giving it to the Senior Operations Managers. The Senior Operations Managers planned the whole year in advance in terms of meetings, special events, weekly cadences, and offsite outings. They taught the leadership classes during the All Leader Meetings. I had capable leaders at all levels whom I trusted to deliver results and deliver them the right way. I knew I would not be the leader of this DC my whole career because that would not be fair to my team; they deserved to lead the building/team themselves.

Several big events occurred that, had we still been the old team with the old mindset, we might not have survived. There were three hurricanes that impacted our customers and the community. There were major, whole operation shut-downs that occurred due to the age of the building which required months of planning and detailed execution. The unemployment rate was at an all-time low, which increased turnover within the building because hourly team members could more easily job-jump to different companies. Despite these setbacks, the team successfully pushed through to the end of the third year and my final few months with the company. I was proud of my team and our remarkable achievements!

A few years after I moved on from the team, the world experienced COVID-19, which is arguably the most disruptive event in any of our lifetimes. All the difficult times experienced by the team made them stronger to successfully navigate operating in a pandemic environment. During the pandemic I reached out to several of my leaders and team members to check on them, and all of them indicated they were adequately prepared to handle the changes because of the transformational process they went through several years prior.

KEY TAKEAWAYS OF CHAPTER 2:

Touched only briefly on the turnaround, because I will go into more detail in the following chapters, but I want to share how far this team of 850 team members and 60 leaders came in three years. Although I orchestrated the three-year process, the truth is that it was successful because the leaders and hourly team members changed the way they traditionally thought, and they were able to believe in the vision we developed together. Below is a list of our accomplishments, and this team continues to be a shining star for the company.

1. OSHA Rate was 14% when I came to the team. The maximum number of consecutive safe days the building went in 15 years was 144 when it first opened. On the day I left, the OSHA rate was less than .75% and they had not had an injury for 177 days.

2. P&L Performance. Over the first 15 years, the team had struggled to come in under budget on Cost Per Case Shipped (SG&A), but since then, the team has been at or under budget for three years in a row, thus saving the company money.

3. Hourly team member incentive made up of performance and quality was at $.05 per hour worked when I came to the team. The maximum amount is $1.10 that an hourly team member can make on their quarterly paycheck based on the number of hours

worked. This meant each team member missed out on over $2,000 per year because we could not perform the basics of the business correctly. The day I left; the team had earned $1.00 per hour worked. There was still room for improvement, but imagine what that did for the morale of the team members who had been a part of the team when they were earning only $.05.

4. Performance of Case Per Man Hour (CPH) measured how many cases could enter and leave the building using the least amount of labor hours possible. This had a major impact on the P&L. The team performed 150 CPH when I got there and could not understand how they could perform any better than that. When I left, the team was operating at 190 CPH consistently with few to no additional technological improvements. In fact, the technology brought into the building actually did not work and negatively impacted the performance of the team, yet they overcame that obstacle as well.

5. There were 650 hourly team members and 53 leaders when I joined the team. Three years later, there were 850 hourly team members and 60 leaders.

6. The Playbook we developed was implemented in two other buildings within the division, making those teams better.

7. Most importantly, considering all the metric-type improvements that help the company in the long run, the team had turned into a "Leadership Factory." There were three types of leadership development programs: the first was called the Path to Leadership Program which was designed for hourly team members looking to get into entry-level management. The second was the Area Leader High Potential Program (we called "Ghost Squad") created for new leaders to strengthen their abilities, and the third

was an Eagle Elite Training Program for hourly team members to learn how to properly train our new hires and team members trying to make a job transition. Over 16 hourly team members were promoted to Area Leader either to our team or other teams within the company, six Area Leaders were promoted to Senior Leader roles within our Team or other teams within the company, and two Senior Leaders were promoted to my peer level within the company. This is what being a good leader is all about—making the lives of those who trust in you better.

8. The Team got even better after I left. One mark of a great leader is how well your team continues to do after you leave. The following year, they earned Safety DC of the Year and continue to thrive.

CHAPTER THREE:

TRUST & CREDIBILITY

"Without trust we don't truly collaborate; we merely coordinate or, at best, cooperate. It is trust that transforms a group of people into a team."

~Stephen M.R. Covey

TRUST AND CREDIBILITY are the foundations of leadership. This concept is discussed at length by Kouzes and Posner in their book, *The Leadership Challenge*.[1] I could not agree with them more, which is why this is always the FIRST step to take in building a team, regardless of size. This phase can take a long time depending on the previous culture of the team. If the leader hears, "You are the fifth leader to come to this team and say things will be different and nothing ever changes," prepare for a long road because there is so much distrust within the culture. Think about life: If a trusted parent said he/she was going to do something and that parent did not follow through, how would that feel? A request might be made again, but with hesitancy. If this continued to occur, it would be difficult to ever trust that parent.

Trust: assured reliance on the character, ability, strength, or truth of some-one or something.[2]

Credibility: the quality or power of inspiring belief.[3]

Analogy: Funding the Credibility Bank

I like the idea of a "Credibility Bank"[4]; every time you, as a leader, do something you say you will do, you make a small deposit into the bank. Every time you fail to do what others expect of you, there is a massive withdrawal. In terms of money, a swipe of the debit card and the cash is immediately taken out of a bank account; however, in order to deposit money into the account, the owner must wait at least two weeks for an employer to deposit the hard-earned money into the account. Credibility is no different. You cannot immediately earn the trust back once a withdrawal is taken from your credibility by not doing something you said you would do. It will take several deposits of earning trust to fill the bank account back up to operating levels. Doing what you say you will do is critical to properly building a team. This a major step in the Forming Phase (of the Four Stages of Team Development).

With this being such a delicate balance, what is the secret to success to build trust and credibility? It is actually very simple: DO WHAT YOU SAY YOU ARE GOING TO DO and lead with transparency. There is always a power struggle of knowledge. Whoever has the knowledge has the power. Why is that? Because a leader thinks the "lower level" team members can't handle it? Yet, every book talks about empowering team members. Do not be afraid to be transparent with the team unless it is something personal or if the timing is not right because it could severely impact the operation or financial stability of the team. A leader is not always smarter than the team members, so why not have them help with the challenges faced.

When I first joined the Eagles team, I made it a point to always carry my "To-Do List," which was a typed outline of what I planned to do that day with several open slots available for additions to the list. Carrying my list, I walked the DC floor where the team members were hauling freight, picking cases, leading, or fixing things. I made eye contact with team members and asked how they were doing and if there was anything I could do to help—no matter how easy or difficult. If they asked me for a pencil, I would immediately get one for them. If they had frustrations with how the operation was being performed, I listened for as long as it took while taking notes. When it was a complex issue, I was honest and told them it would not get fixed immediately, but I made note of it. Every time I saw that team member, I told them I did not forget, but it was still not the right time. I ultimately checked the request off my to-do list by either doing as they asked or following up with an explanation as to WHY we could not accomplish their request.

For example, my lift driver teammate made a comment about communication within the team being a major issue. Teammates were spread throughout the million-square good DC, and this particular teammate believed it was inefficient to track down a leader in order to get something done for his/her job. Communication is a major hurdle in any team and can be extremely difficult to manage. I informed the team member that I would look into it and get back to him. Because of the previous culture, he did not believe a word I said. And why should he? I was just another leader trying to tell the team members what he wanted to hear in order to move on with my day. It took four months to get something implemented because it was truly complex, but meanwhile, every time I saw that particular team member, I thanked him for sparking a good idea that would help the efficiency within the building and help improve the team.

To solve the problem, I gathered a few leaders to talk through it together. These leaders had each been in the building for more than 10 years, so had a lot of experience to draw from. At that time, frontline leaders carried radios to communicate, but each radio cost $500, which was too much money to pay to give one to each of the 20 lift drivers on an operational shift. That price seemed absurd to me, so I asked why we paid that much. And I got a response of, "That's what we have always paid this vendor." I asked a lot of questions to get to a better answer:

- Why do we use this vendor?

- Can we use another vendor?

- What prevents us from using a different vendor?

- Are there cheaper radios out there in the marketplace?

- Will the thick building walls or metal interfere with the frequency?

- Will the freezing temperatures within the ice cream room impact the radios?

Ultimately, we found a company that made inexpensive radios that cost $10 each. I purchased 10 of them to test out. I gave the first one to the team member who originally brought it to my attention to get his feedback after testing the radio. This showed that, not only had I listened to him, but I wanted him to be a part of the solution. The radios worked well. I will talk more about the next steps in the chapter on Structure & Organization, but to quickly summarize, I wrote a Standard Operating Procedure on the checkout and maintenance/charging procedures for the radios. This ensured accountability for the radios for all shifts within the DC. Ultimately, this led to other departments obtaining similar radios for better communication in their day-to-day operations. The result of this new program was more than just improved communication, performance, morale, and safety; it was a huge credibility deposit and trust boost.

Every time I told the leaders I would do something, I made sure I did it, or explained why I could not. I was transparent and forthcoming about everything possible. Eventually, the leaders began to pick up on this and imitated the behavior with the team members on the team. Every time I did what I was asked, a small deposit was made into my credibility bank. This impacted morale in a positive way and allowed me to make the changes needed for the future.

ALONG THE WAY: SOME THINGS TO WATCH OUT FOR

It sounds so simple: "Do what you say you are going to do." In reality, this is not so simple, especially if the previous culture was destroyed by distrust. You, as a leader, must not assume people will trust you because you are a great, fun, lovable person. You must be intentional about building trust.[5]

This takes a lot of time and energy. The size of the team impacts the complexity; the more team members who are asking questions or asking for things, the more difficult it is to keep track of all the requests and "go dos." Being new to the team and having to learn the names of so many individuals adds to the difficulty. Do not be afraid to ask a team member his/her name. The team members do not expect the new leader to remember 50-900 names in the first week. They do, however, expect the leader to fulfill his/her commitment to them. This is where having some sort of tracking method is critical. The daily checklist I printed out ensured that I could always write down the names of the team members, their requests, and dates I talked to them.

By the end of the day rule: Time management

The overall company culture encouraged leaders to always provide a response to team members in a timely manner. It was believed that if a team member asked a leader a question, the leader owed a response to the team member by the next day. Now, sometimes the request required more time (like in the case of the lift driver and the poor communication), but the leader owed a response to inform the team member of the time frame in which to expect an answer. This is a great rule for any company or team to follow.

I quickly realized that not all leaders exhibit good time management or organizational management. This made it difficult to manage a response to a team member who asked for something. The thought of doing a daily checklist really bothered some of my leaders, so it was important to develop a tool for them to encourage the adherence to the company rule and more importantly, take care of their teammates. Eventually, when the team was further into the journey, the leaders and I developed a tiny notebook that broke down (by quarter) everything a leader needed to know on a daily/weekly/monthly basis. It included a section for taking notes on the requests of team members. I wanted it embedded in the culture that all the positive momentum gained could be lost in an instant with the loss of credibility with the team members. It was not okay to get comments from team members who said their leaders never did what they said they were going to do. This notebook was a tool that worked for some leaders, but not others. Ultimately, each leader must utilize what works best for them.

TEAM SIZE MATTERS: COMPLEXITY WITH LARGER TEAMS
Complexity is added when the team is large with many shifts or when team members are in different geographical locations. The leader must be intentional about making time for his/her team members. Not only do you, as a leader, need to be physically available to team members, you must be in your team's environment because when you are the "boss" your rank can be intimidating. This might not seem like a big deal to you, but to those team members who see upper management only once in a while, it is a big deal. Do not overlook the point that rank or title—whether a leader likes it or not—carries a lot of weight. The team member is not likely to go to a leader's office on his/her own to address a problem, ask a question, or offer a suggestion. Interactions occur because the leader took the time to be intentionally present in the environment of the team member.

Try it a few times; walk into the environment of a team member, spend time asking questions, and really be present. That team member will tell five other team members, who will tell five more team members. Eventually, team members will start engaging the leader to see if it is true. "Will he really do what he says he will do? Will she really engage with me?" It is crucial that a leader not look at her watch every two minutes to indicate she has to be moving on, or worse, walk the other way when she sees a team member coming up to talk to her.

You will notice over time that the trust begins to grow, and the credibility builds. This is a good way to build up credit in your Credibility Bank or, failing to do so, withdraw from it. Constant engagement is powerful and extremely impactful. Do not make the mistake, in the first several months of joining a team, of staying in your office to try to dig into the numbers because you think that will solve team problems. Nothing in the rest of this book will work without taking as much time as necessary to get this trust component right. People ask all the time, "How long will it take to turn the team around?" That is a loaded question because this phase of trust building is so delicate. It was never just about me building trust and credibility with my team members. I needed to build it with my leaders, model the way it is done, and then ensure that my leaders exhibited those same actions and behaviors. I could have made a personal impact by building all the trust and credibility for myself, but if my frontline team members did not trust the leaders within my team, there would still be a disconnect and distrust, especially after I moved on.

TOUGH CHOICES: WITH WHOM DO I BUILD TRUST FIRST?

A big question at the beginning of the team-building phase is, "With whom do I spend my initial time building trust: the frontline team members or direct leaders who interact daily with the team members conducting the actual work?" Ideally, a leader needs to do both simultaneously, but from a practical standpoint, one group will get the most attention in the beginning. I do not believe there is a right answer to this, and many leaders might disagree with my approach, but I chose to spend my initial time with my Eagles leaders. I wanted them to know my leadership philosophy and team-building strategy, to think of themselves as LEADERS, not managers, and I wanted them to know the "why" behind everything we did.

I learned in the military to have high expectations of the teams I led. In order to have a high-performance team, the leaders need to hold themselves to a higher standard than the team members they lead. I found the best way to do this was to have a "Leadership Contract."

PUT IT IN WRITING: LEADERSHIP CONTRACT

Having a Leadership Contract is something I learned in the military, confirmed in a leadership book, and decided to implement early in my career. This was fundamental to my leadership style of building trust and credibility. Below are four of the most important principles I led by (out of 10). There is an example of a Leadership Contract I used with my leaders in the Appendix.

1. Set the right example for my team by my own actions in all things.

2. Be fair, impartial, and consistent in matters relating to work, rules, discipline, and rewards.

3. Make sure the team members always know in advance what I expect from them in the way of conduct and performance on the job.

4. Show the team that I can "do" as well as "lead" by pitching in to work beside them when my help is needed.

If you, as the leader, try to manage from behind your "rank on a collar," not model the way and point versus show, it will be a very long road for you, and the end state will ultimately be failure. Leadership is about influence, and a leader influences by setting the right example in all areas of life. Be consistent in decision-making. The right decision might not always be made, but a leader must be fair and consistent with those he/she serves and leads. Expectations must be clear in advance; this is what this section is all about. A team member should not have to guess or try to read the mind of the leader to decipher what is important and what is not.

During my initial sit-down with team members, I tried to create a comfortable environment for them where I could get to know them as individuals. I do not recall where I heard this, but I do believe it: a leader can only effectively get to know between five to seven individuals. By effectively, I mean the leader knows the teammate's spouse's name, dog's name, interests, hobbies, etc. I would write down their answers to the questions I had for them:

1. What do you like/not like about the team so far?

2. Tell me your story. How did you get to where you are today?

3. What are you passionate about? What are your hobbies?

4. What are the names of your family members? What do they do?

5. What do you expect from me as your leader?

6. Where do you want your career to go within the next five years?

7. What is an area of your life you would like an opportunity to improve?

After I get to know them and have many notes I can reference in the future, I slide my Leadership Contract over to them. I cover each of my 10 leadership principles and explain why I believe these are important. I start the conversation by stating, "I know the standards I have for the team are high, but it is my belief that the standard you have for me should be even higher. I will cover my leadership principles and expect you to hold me to these. I expect that if you see me not living these principles on a daily basis to address it with me." At the end, I give them a chance to ask any follow-up questions, and I ask them to sign the document. I also sign the document and explain that it does not go in their file; it is only referenced as a contract between two people. It makes it formal and real for accountability purposes, but not intimidating. I scanned the copies and saved them on my computer in a folder.

After these conversations, I am under a microscope at all times. Team members watched me to see if I meant what I said. Was I truly modeling these principles, or was that just a stunt to gain their approval? This exercise did more for building trust and credibility than anything else I did. It worked because I modeled my beliefs. It worked because I didn't do it to gain favor with the team; I did it because I truly believed in what I was saying, and I was taking ownership of how the team should act.

It should not end here. Everything a leader does should be about his/her principles. Do not spend an hour getting to know a team member on an individual level and then never ask again about his/her family. Here is a tip: people do not want to talk about work or job performance. Teammates want to brag about their grandchildren and family. They want to talk about their passions. This is what they care about, which is great. I know it is important to talk about the performance of the team and what the team member needs to do in order to make the team better, but to get to their hearts a leader must talk to them about other areas of their lives.

Remember their kids' names. Wish them "Happy Birthday!" If remembering 50 birthdays is hard, then I suggest using technology to provide the reminders. The team members do not care how a leader remembers their birthdays, just that there was effort. Make it a point to follow up with team members about events in their lives. If a team member has a kid who had a baseball game, write a note to ask them how he/she did in the game during the next interaction. These little gestures do wonders to build credibility. This is ongoing and should outlast the first few months of joining the team. The leader must embody this behavior. This helps define the leader in the eyes of the team members, and—oh, by the way—the leader's leaders will start to model this habit because the team members will be vocal with their direct leaders on how this made them feel because it made them feel good. It made them feel valued and important.

IT IS ALL MARKETING: LEADERSHIP BRAND

When I led the Eagles, there were things I did on a consistent basis to ensure my credibility, and they were part of my leadership brand. Everyone has a "brand" in how they show up in the world. A personal brand is usually something someone is passionate about or strongly believes. It is how the individual wants the world to view them. I certainly believed strongly in leadership, so most of my interactions with people in the world revolve around the importance of leaders to a team. I cared about whether or not my team members believed I was genuine and truly cared. I inserted all the birthdays of my leaders into the Microsoft Outlook calendar so I was notified of their special day. I called the leaders on the phone if they were not in the office, and let them know I was thinking of them and wished them a great day. It was a simple and impactful gesture, which took little effort. In addition, I wrote 10-15 handwritten notes per month to random team members. I sent the notes to their homes, so they could share the moments with their loved ones. The letters were not generic notes; they were specific to that team member and the impact they made.

Here are some ideas that cost nothing but have a high impact:

1. Handwritten notes

2. Birthday wishes

3. Public recognition in front of peers (also note that some individuals do not like public recognition)

4. Adjusting your schedule to interact with different team members every day

5. Write a simple email

6. If you run into a team member in town, make it a point to brag about them in front of their loved ones

The bottom line is that once a commitment is made to a Leadership Contract, the leader must take ownership in modeling the behaviors because teammates are watching. This should be an easy task if the leader truly believes in the values in his/her contract and it fits their personal brand.

GETTING STARTED: SETTING INITIAL EXPECTATIONS

After you, as the leader, provide your leadership contract, you can now schedule a follow-up, sit-down conversation with the same individuals to discuss what you specifically expect from the team member. Many leaders of teams fail because they do not provide simple and clear expectations of each team member. It must be part of the process to sit down with all direct reports in a safe environment in order to cover the expectations for each person, even if the expectations are all the same. A safe environment might be an office, but it should be a location that makes the team member feel comfortable opening up and potentially being vulnerable. The leader should document (no more than two pages) the expectations of that individual in great detail. It is not necessary to read directly from the document, as this becomes too scripted. The leader can highlight key points to discuss and make the interaction more conversational. Ensure there is clarity around the talking points. The team member must never leave the conversation confused or unclear as to what the leader expects from him/

her. Do not make the document a list of "dos" and "don'ts"; break the document down in terms of personal, professional, key performance indicators, leadership, teammate, growth, and development. If the team member challenges a point, explain the "why" behind it or remove it from the document if there is no alignment. Research professor and vulnerability expert, Brené Brown says, "To be clear is to be kind, and to be unclear is to be unkind."[6] If you are not kind with clarity, you cannot build trust.

Ultimately, the team members sign the document, receive a copy, and strive to achieve the goals agreed upon. This same document helps to track progress and act as a guide during professional coaching sessions, such as mid-year and annual evaluations. A team member should not end the year with any surprises during the annual evaluation and feedback process. A surprised team member means the leader did not do a good job of coaching or failed to provide clarity in the discussions with the team member. In essence, the leader failed to build trust.

The direct reports need to take their signed, initial expectation-setting documents and produce another similar document for their own direct team members. This new document should align to the original document, but add specific details regarding the particular area of the business they oversee. The process is the same for this relationship. Once all leaders and team members conduct sit-down conversations, everyone on the team knows what is expected.

A key point many leaders miss is following through on setting the initial expectations. If, after the initial brief from one leader to another, none of the other leaders set the expectations with their own team members, then everyone on the team would be held to a different standard, which does not bode well for trust and can, in fact, actually hurt a team. It not only creates distrust of the senior leader, but it builds distrust among team members because the team is moving in different directions. So, you, as the main leader, must "inspect what you expect"[7] as Dave Ramsey says, by ensuring that all conversations are conducted in the same way. You can ask questions of other leaders and team members as a test to ensure they understand the expectations. This will ensure that everyone is on the same page, and if some members of the team are not, then at least you know and can correct it.

ANNUAL EVALUATION: ONE-ON-ONE WITH TEAM MEMBERS

Part of the process of building trust and credibility is setting expectations early, letting the team know what is expected, and also providing proper feedback and coaching. After the initial expectations are set, the coaching and teaching begins. Setting clear expectations is important, but if the leader does not follow up with feedback throughout the year, it could result in a difficult conversation when the annual evaluation occurs. Too many leaders are afraid of hurting someone's feelings by providing constructive feedback. There is a right way to give feedback and a wrong way. A teammate should leave a coaching session energized to improve, not defeated and down. With that being said, a leader must provide absolute clarity around what the teammate is doing well (keep doing) and where he/she is not meeting the expectation (change/adjust). No one is perfect, and hopefully, the leader hires people who care about self-improvement. Everyone has a different personality and some people do not handle feedback well, but feedback is critical to a high-performing team. This is why the annual evaluation is such a critical part of trust building and where many companies fail miserably. I am sure the reader has received an annual evaluation from a boss at some point that went like this:

SITUATION:

Team Member Perspective: The team member has been waiting in anticipation for the conversation (annual evaluation) for 10 months because he/she thinks they did an outstanding job this year. The team member thinks it is the best year he/she has had in their career. They think their boss is going to sing their praises and tell them the company would go under if they were not on the team.

Boss Perspective: The boss cannot believe it is already the end of the year. He/she does not have time to sit down with 10 leaders to tell them how they performed. He/she just wants to give everyone an average rating to minimize the work because he/she cannot be expected to remember all the things each one did for the whole year. He/she cannot believe the company makes leaders fill out this lame form for Human Resources. He/she decides to make it general for all team members and then copy and paste similar responses.

ANNUAL EVALUATION:

Boss in Meeting: "Thanks for coming in Bob. I apologize we are just sitting down now two months into the next year, but you know how Corporate is, we finally finished calibration." Boss slides the company evaluation form across the desk to you.

Boss says, "You will notice many of the comments in there are what you wrote about yourself. I think you had a really good year and the team is lucky to have you. You will see you received an average rating (Solid). You should be really proud of this. Read through the evaluation and let me know if you have any questions.

Team Member in Meeting: The team member has mixed emotions and can barely speak because this is not exactly what he/she thought would happen. The team member is scared to tell his/her boss they disagree because he/she has to continue earning a living and make money.

Team Member says, "No, I do not have any questions."

Boss in Meeting: Boss shares with the team member the increase in pay and how much more money he/she would be making if he/she were to receive an above average rating instead. The boss thanks the team member for all their 365 days of work within this 10-minute time period, and tells them he/she will see them out there.

Team Member Emotions: The team member is so angry; they are not sure what to do. He/she starts questioning what they are doing in life, if they are at the right company, and if they are truly valued by those they work with. The team member gets on LinkedIn to look for other jobs with other companies. The team member is confused and unsure what they did right or wrong.

This may not be a familiar scenario for you personally, but I have actually experienced it several times in the workplace. There is a disconnect between what the leader thinks and what the teammate thinks. This is not a good experience, and–as a result–these companies will experience higher turnover, unmotivated employees, and slower growth.

I took a very different approach to annual evaluations, which I learned from my time in the military and improved upon throughout my time at the company. Beware, the process you are going to read about is painfully time-consuming and mentally draining, but so worth it. As the leader of the Eagles, I had 12 direct reports that worked hard for me over a 12-month time period. I had extremely high expectations for them within the company, and my leaders were rock stars. It took me at least six hours per leader to prepare for each 90-120-minute long evaluation—a feedback session which each leader DESERVED. Preparation started the previous year with the initial expectation-setting meeting discussed earlier. Then, I blocked off time each month to take notes on each leader. This way, I kept track of all the things my team members did in the beginning, middle, and end of the year. So many times leaders forget things that happened in the early part of the year which might have been significant.

I planned out everything I wanted to discuss as it related to the leader's performance, the performance of the team, status of the goals of the team, personal growth, strengths, areas to improve, and financials. I built in time for the team members to talk about how they felt the past year went (An example of a flow I used can be found in the Appendix). I used the agreed-upon Key Performance Indicators (KPIs) from the beginning of the year, and made a simple Excel sheet that tracked the performance by Month/Quarter/Year. This showed the ups and downs. For me, in an operational role, we had metrics around Safety (OSHA), labor hours (cases in and out of the building), quality, turnover, P&L performance, leadership accountability, growth of other leaders, and engagement. This same concept is beneficial in any corporate environment as long as everyone involved understands the KPIs and targets.

I printed everything out and placed the documents in a folder the leader could take when the conversation was completed. I, of course, had used all the data and inputs to write the formal annual evaluation the company required me to give. This was a small portion of the conversation. It was important to properly complete it because it coincided with financial incentives, so it was a big deal, but I made it clear with the other documents and conversation how I came to the final rating.

The evaluation document laid out the details of the year for each team member. I provided specific examples, his/her rating, strengths, areas to improve, projects he/she worked on, and the expectations for the following year. This is the document I used to guide the conversation. It provided several opportunities for the leader to ask questions, provide his/her own input, and engage in meaningful feedback. At the end of the evaluation conversation, I thanked him/her for the hard work and dedication to the vision of the team. I encouraged the leader to take care of his/her own leaders by providing a similar structure. I offered to sit in on evaluations with my leader's direct reports if he/she desired. I found out afterwards that more than 80% of the leaders utilized a similar structure to conduct the annual evaluation and provide end of the year feedback.

MAIN GOAL: TRUST & CREDIBILITY CLOSING

I had a mission to create a "Leadership Factory" on the team because I wanted to promote my teammates. I encouraged teammates to step outside their comfort zones, and I'm sure I sounded like a broken record with this line, "My job is not to make you a better leader for this company only. My job is to make you a better leader, period. If you want to go to a different company for an opportunity I cannot provide, then do it. The thing I care about most is, when you leave, can you tell me you are a better leader for being on this team? If the answer is yes, then the effort was a success." That is what taking care of people is all about, not, "I will only take care of you if you stay on my team." That is one-sided and people eventually see right through that.

There are many examples used in this chapter of what practices enabled me to build trust and credibility with my Eagles team. It does not matter if you lead a warehouse, manufacturing plant, marketing team, finance team, or consulting company, the initial step is to build trust and credibility. It becomes the foundation for accomplishing anything with a team. People do not come to work every day determined to do a bad job. Assume positive intent on the part of those on the team. Motivational speaker and business consultant Marcus Buckingham said, "People leave managers, not companies." Over time, these people, who once had positive intent, lose trust in their leadership team for not doing the little things mentioned in this chapter. It is important to understand that this is something the leader has control over. The leader has the ability to set the foundation and tone. The next chapter is about vision and goal setting; will team members follow a vision and care about team goals if they don't trust the leader? No. Every chapter I present in this book comes back to this concept.

KEY TAKEAWAYS OF CHAPTER 3:

1. Do what you say you are going to do. Not following up is detrimental to your credibility.

2. You cannot get through the Forming Stage of the Four Stages of Team Development without trust and credibility (more on the Four Stages of Team Development later in the book).

3. Engage your team in their environment. Do not make the individual come to your environment (office). Be aware of the rank you hold because although you might not care about your rank within the company, it carries a lot of weight and can intimidate team members.

4. Provide clarity with your expectations:
   a. Get to know your team members on a personal level (Document this).
   b. Provide a "Leadership Contract" of what you, as the leader, believe (brand leadership).
   c. Set initial expectations in a comfortable environment that clearly defines expectations.
   d. Document the progress of the team members throughout the year.
   e. Follow up with teammates by providing direct feedback/ coaching before mid-year and annual evaluations.

5. Take the time to provide productive and detailed annual evaluations to your team members that show their hard work meant something and added value.

CHAPTER FOUR:

VISION & GOAL SETTING

"Visions thrive in an environment of unity; they die in an environment of division."

~ Andy Stanley

STRATEGIES, MISSION STATEMENTS, visions, goals, objectives, and values are all words companies use to try to define their "culture." Corporate headquarters or warehouses have the company values and beliefs stenciled on the walls. A visitor might think, "Wow, those are really good and inspiring. This is a place I could work and really fit in." And then the visitor starts to interact with the employees at the company and something does not add up. The visitor saw "Respect for the Individual" emblazoned above the reception desk, but witnessed a person giving a speech while half the employees were on phones or talking to each other, which seemed extremely disrespectful. Or, when the visitor walks into the building, a large sign says, "SAFETY IS THE NUMBER ONE THING WE CARE ABOUT," but within 10 minutes of walking the operational floor, he/she sees more unsafe acts than safe behaviors. Did those employees not read the sign when walking into the building?

Or perhaps, there is a mission statement written in calligraphy in the conference room, yet not one person in the whole building could recite it from memory (It's only 10 words). If these scenarios resonate, know that signage is a great idea in theory, and that many leadership authors address this very topic. BUT, a vision pasted on a wall or value statements hanging on the door do not motivate a team member to adhere to these ideals. It is a process that takes a lot of time. Just like building trust and credibility, developing a vision that everyone believes in takes time, energy, and repetition. The majority of team members need to be involved in the development of the vision, and the majority of team members MUST know what the vision actually is; otherwise, it will just be words on a wall with no meaning.

PUT IT IN WRITING: SETTING FORTH THE VISION

When I believed I had built significant trust with the Eagles leaders, I took one step further in our journey by establishing a vision. I "prepped the battlefield"[1] for several weeks by talking about the concept of a vision in every meeting I had with the leaders in the DC. I reminded them of the steps the team had taken to make the progress they made in the past several months, and I explained the importance behind the momentum gained. Next, I scheduled a whole-day meeting with the senior leaders. I informed them ahead of time that the meeting would be long and to plan accordingly with their leaders and families. The meeting agenda included the following topics: vision and goal setting, how to develop a vision, how to set goals for the year, and how to develop bold initiatives. I explained that the purpose of the meeting was to produce:

1. The Eagles Vision (which would not change over the years)

2. Ten SMART Goals that drive the business for the year

3. Five to eight Initiatives to help the team achieve the 10 goals

4. Two to three group projects that would add value to the business

Andy Stanley is a pastor in Atlanta and a world-renowned speaker on leadership. He wrote a book called *Visioneering*, which I used to teach my leaders. To me, the vision becomes our North Star through which decisions should be made. Even when we get knocked off course and disheartening things happen within the business, the North Star is always there to guide us and get us back on track as long as we understand where the team is going. I called this the "Roadmap to Success." I told my leaders, "Leaders create and cast a compelling vision and mobilize individuals to fulfill a vision. That is the role of a leader: they design the path, they communicate the directions clearly, and they lead their team toward that preferred future with little deviation."

The vision started with the senior leaders. If they understood its importance, then we could model the way it should be brought to life and have the vision infiltrate all levels of the team. Jim Collins, American researcher and business consultant, uses the analogy of "The Bus." The bus represents the company, which is (hopefully) moving in a positive direction. Collins's idea is to get the right people on the bus, sitting in the right seats, or—more literally—to hire the right people for the company and make sure they are performing the jobs they are qualified for. I like to add that it is also important to establish who is driving the bus. If you have the right people on the bus but the driver is lost or driving off a cliff, then the proper placement of riders does not matter. I was adamant that I did not want the team built around me. I did not want to be the driver of the bus, the team, or the business because the vision then becomes a matter of, "We are only doing this because Patrick said so," resulting in zero ownership. We will talk about the importance of ownership later, but the team had to be built around the vision, not one individual. This is true for any type of team. This is true for a young couple starting a family, a coach of a sports team, leader of a marketing team, or manager of an operations team. The vision helps to drive the culture, personality, attitude, and desires of the team.

It was important for the leaders on the team to stop waiting for guidance from me on everything and start taking initiative. The problem with taking initiative is that all the leaders must have clarity about their left and right limits (military language for "parameters"). As long as the goals they set align with the established vision, then it is the right initiative to take. I wanted them to take risks, and I let them know that it was okay to fail. I told the following story in our meeting:

> *There is no decision you can make that will break the building. We can fix just about anything. I want you to treat this building and this team like a playground. Kids may fall off the monkey bars, scrape their knees and elbows on the asphalt, and on rare occasions break an arm, but they learn from these mistakes and failures. They learn not to stand on top of the monkey bars or jump off the slide because they can fall and get hurt. I want you to take chances in the operation. If you make a decision, and it was the wrong decision, learn from it and make a better decision the next time. I would rather you failed because you tried something, than play it conservative and never get off the safe bench. Treat the building like a playground and we will be just fine. And most importantly we will grow as a team and move the business forward.*

At the beginning of the meeting, I recapped the events from the previous year since I joined the team. I explained the behaviors I had noticed. I provided clarity on what I expected from the team for the upcoming year to set the tone and direction. Below are the some of the things I wanted the team to think about when developing a vision:

1. Integrity in everything we do

2. Drive the safety culture

3. Drive team member engagement

4. Provide customer service

5. Professionalism

6. Leader and hourly team member development

7. Expense control. Treat the P&L as if it were your own checkbook

8. Innovation and excellence in our business

9. Communication

I explained during the meeting:

> *Vision gives significance to the otherwise meaningless details of our business. Team, we are shipping cases. It's not rocket science. Let's face it, much of what we do doesn't appear to matter much on a large scale, but take the minutiae of the everyday battle, stir it, and you have purpose, meaning, and momentum. The end state is what matters. All your hard work, long hours, and time away from your families boils down to whether or not we fulfilled our vision. Vision evokes passion and emotion, provides motivation to complete the mundane tasks of our day-to-day operation, and most importantly, it provides direction by serving as a "Roadmap for Success," translating into purpose.*

There are many comparisons in books about "vision setting." I prefer the analogy of the North Star. A vision should act as the North Star and provide direction for the team. Even if you do not know the path forward or the obstacles you will face, if you look up in the sky, the North Star lets you know if you are going the right direction. Imagine it was a cloudy night and you could not see the North Star. If you did not have a compass or a vision, how would you know if you were going the correct way? Think about the companies that operate with a vision where fewer than half the people truly understand it. Half the company is going one direction and the other half is going another direction. How will anything be accomplished? These companies are unlikely to reach their true potential for success. When everyone believes in the words that are on the wall because they understand the meaning and how to articulate the vision, then leaders and teammates can make decisions about the best direction the team needs to take. Sometimes it does not matter if the team goes left or right, but it does matter how to get pointed back toward the North Star/vision. I used this analogy to explain the importance, not just of developing a vision, but also of how to establish the "right" vision.

It really surprised me that the Eagles team had not had a vision in all 15 years since the building was built. Every team member had a different view of what purpose they served. Below is a list of successful companies and their established visions.[2]

- **IKEA**: "Our vision is to create a better everyday life for many people."

- **Nike**: "Bring inspiration and innovation to every athlete* in the world"

- **Patagonia**: "Build the best product, cause no unnecessary harm, use business to inspire and implement solutions to the environmental crisis."

What do you notice about these visions? They are broad, yet directional. They are short, taking fewer than 12 words. You can imagine setting goals and initiatives to achieve them. They tell the "why" versus the "what." If you have never read Simon Sinek's *Start with Why*, I highly recommend it. As Sinek says, "People don't care what you do. They care why you do it."[3] It is much easier to get your team to believe in a vision when they understand how the vision came to be and why it is so important.

During the meeting with the leaders, some of them really grasped the idea and got energized by it, while others were hesitant and were only "going through the motions." This is completely normal. Setting a vision with a team that just learned the idea and never had one before is a major change, and as I am sure you already know, change is hard and is often met with resistance. Just because a leader is met with resistance does not mean he/she is wrong for wanting to change. Despite the resistance, I still needed to complete the exercise and ensure the vision created had the input and voice of each leader on the team.

After seven hours in the meeting, the team had created a vision to withstand the test of time, set 10 goals for the year geared toward the vision, and created 10 initiatives to achieve these goals. By the end of the meeting, the most resistant leader of the group had made a suggestion to have the vision and goals put on an employee badge backer for all to reference, which was a great idea. Every team member had to carry their employee identification badge, so by making the vision and goals the same size made it easy to attach and reference at all times. This was the vision created by the team:

PROVIDE A SAFE, RESULTS-DRIVEN ATMOSPHERE BUILT UPON INTEGRITY, TEAMWORK, AND PROFESSIONALISM

BACK TO BASICS: UNPACKING THE VISION

We started developing this vision by discussing what–in their minds– were the most important values for the business. For the past five years, the building had the worst safety behaviors as measured by OSHA in the company supply chain. This meant that, out of more than 80 distribution centers with similar structures to ours, we were near the bottom, if not at the very bottom. By structure, I am referring to DCs that delivered grocery products and general merchandise. To give you an idea, the industry average for an OSHA violation rate was ~3%. The building we created a vision for had an OSHA rate of 15%: every 10 days an hourly team member was injured and sought medical attention. Naturally, the leaders thought safety should be a top priority for the team. I will discuss this later when we put it all together, but many times, poor safety behaviors are an indicator of poor leadership.

There were many different types of personalities in the room, but there were some senior leaders who served within the company for at least 15 years and in this same building their whole careers who hated being last in performance and efficiency. In operations such as distribution centers, everything is measured as a cost. Operations do not actually make the company any money. There are no goods or products sold at the warehouse, so efficiency and cutting costs out of the operation become extremely important. There are several key performance indicators (KPIs) the company used to measure performance, and they ranked each distribution center accordingly. Out of 40 grocery distribution centers, the Eagles' operational performance ranked 39th. Sure, the leaders provided many excuses about how their building was different from the other buildings in the network. In my short career with the company, I had been in four different buildings and leaders in each one said the same thing, "Our building and team are just different. The company leadership just does not understand." Needless to say, my leaders were tired of being the laughingstock of the network and placed performance as something to strive for in the vision. They used the words "results oriented" to represent this.

Next, the leaders wanted something to set themselves apart from the old culture and old way of doing things in the building. There were 15 years of "shady" things occurring. Outside of the fact that there was zero accountability, there was an extreme lack of character and integrity exhibited by the leaders at the top, which divided the mid-level leaders. For example, there was a "Good Ol' Boys Club" and if you were not a part of it and did not partake in shady dealings, the atmosphere you worked in was one of fear. Now, I come from the military where hanging out with a subordinate alone and not with other team members at a work function was a big "no-no." I learned once I got out that this is not truly the case in the business world, which is fine, but some of the activities on this team crossed the line in my opinion. For example, during the operation, the most senior leader (no longer with the company) would go about 600 yards from the building to hunt deer with a few managers (some still with the company at the time) who were supposed to be working and running the operation. They manipulated numbers to look better than they actually were. They reported these numbers to corporate headquarters, and team members were paid an incentive based upon these manipulated numbers. Now, the team wanted to win, but they wanted to win the right way. This is why they chose "Integrity" as another part of their vision.

Because of the previous poor leadership, the current team was not a team. It was a group of divided individuals who were each out for themselves. Everyone thought they deserved to be promoted because they had tenure. They paid their dues and it was their turn. It was a cutthroat environment and you could see it clearly when you interacted with the team members. The leaders wanted to change that because they felt the only way to win was to draw upon each other's strengths. As a result, "Teamwork" became a pillar of the vision.

Lastly, the team wanted to operate at a different level, and most importantly, did not want to be a one-hit wonder. The leaders wanted to instill this vision into all team members. We were passionate about turning the Eagles into a "Leadership Factory", a place where other leaders sought to come in order to develop and get better. No longer did they want this to be a place that managers left to get away from all the chaos. I say managers because there were few that thought like leaders. It was not their fault. They were never shown the proper way things ought to be done. In addition, they were not developed properly by their own leaders. The leaders who created our vision wanted everyone on the team, all 700 team members (at the time), to carry themselves in a professional way, to stand tall and be proud to be an Eagle. One of my favorite conversations to have with hourly team members occurred when any of them told me they were "just" lift drivers, or "just" orderfillers. I explained to them that each team member has a role on the team. Just because I might have the highest rank does not mean my job or role is any more or less important than theirs. I could never perform their jobs/roles at the same level of efficiency as them. I wanted them to give 100% effort in all they did because that is what I am giving the team every day. In order to develop this level of professionalism, it was going to be imperative to create development programs at all levels within the team. As a result, the leaders decided that the last pillar should be "Professionalism."

After the team members decided on the vision and added their stamp of approval, I provided an example of how we could leverage the vision on a daily basis to provide teachable moments to our other leaders and team members. Not only would this vision become the focus of the discussion at the beginning of every daily meeting, it would be what the leaders would point out to a team member when they operated inside the boundaries and did a great job, as well as when they stepped outside the boundaries and did not meet the necessary expectations.

In our building, the number one safety issue we encountered was "blowing breezeways." This is when a team member on a piece of equipment like a fork lift (that can weigh as much as an F-150 truck) is traveling down an aisle in the warehouse and fails to stop at a cross section. Drivers claim they do this to increase "production" and save time. In reality, it is one of the most dangerous behaviors in a warehouse. Imagine an F-150 traveling 50 mph which does not stop at an intersection on the road and T-bones another car. The result can be catastrophic. These collisions happen in the warehouse as well. This is against company policy and is taught during equipment operations training. Below is an example I used on how to use the vision to teach the team.

> *After witnessing a team member blow a breezeway: I want to talk about how this impacts our vision and what the Eagles are trying to accomplish. Our vision is to provide a safe, results-driven atmosphere, built upon integrity, teamwork, and professionalism. Now, you have a really good chance of hitting another piece of equipment or a pedestrian walking when you blow the breezeway like you just did, which is not very **safe.** If you were to hit someone, this would cause you and the other person to be out of work because*

*you would both be at the hospital, which impacts the performance and **results** within the building. You were trained that this was against company policy when you first joined the company, which impacts your integrity because the definition of **integrity** is doing the right thing even when no one is watching. You are not being a very good **teammate** when you are not thinking about the impact you could have on the rest of the team or their family members. If you were to hit a teammate, you might seriously impact him/her to the point that the teammate could not provide for his/her family. And lastly, not following the rules we have in place to keep the building safe is **unprofessional**. As a result, I will be holding you accountable to this decision and ask you to talk to other teammates about our conversation and be a steward of the vision in the future.*

I showed my leaders how they could use the language of the vision to essentially talk to any team member about anything good or not good that the member was doing. Next, I led the leaders through determining the top 10 goals for the year that would help to fulfill the vision as it was set forth.

TIE IT TO THE VISION: SETTING GOALS

The team created these goals for the first year:

- Goal 1: 2.5 DART/OIR Rate (this was linked to safety)

- Goal 2: Team member incentive: $.80 (this was linked to team member engagement)

- Goal 3: Less than 20% turnover / maintain above 795 staffing

- Goal 4: 170 CPH and ranked 15th or better (this was how the team measured operational performance)

- Goal 5: Quality (.34% cycle, .33% gross, .017% voids) (How the team measured inventory)

- Goal 6: Engagement: earn $25K group VAP, 100% team member relations budget spent, maximize $30.5K Grant contributions, 75 team member VAP participation, 10% or greater commendations given, 72 team member of the month

- Goal 7: 100% audit pass (Food & Health, HR, Maintenance, etc.)

- Goal 8: Customer service: 99.85% outbound Level of service, 92.5% inbound level of service

- Goal 9: Rank top seven in operations index (linked to how the whole distribution center was measured)

- Goal 10: Five internal promotions

To start, we took a brainstorming approach and wrote down as many measurable goals as we could. We did not worry about priority; we focused on specific, measurable, attainable, realistic, and timely (SMART) goals. This might seem like an easy task, but it is important to facilitate the discussions in order to promote engagement from everyone in the room. You really want diversity of thought during this phase of goal setting. It is important to know what stage your team is at, so as to determine the reality of a goal. For example, I had a passionate safety leader (the company called safety leaders the Asset Protection Operations Managers) who was adamant the goal for Safety (OSHA) must be zero injuries requiring medical treatment. The team knew the number one goal should center around safety, but settling on the right metric took almost 90 minutes of back-and-forth discussions. I explained to the safety leader:

> *I loved the goal and the aspiration, and in two years that would be a realistic goal, but right now, at this time, the team has an OSHA rate of 15%, which is 12% higher than the industry average. Going from 15% to 0% is not realistic because it will take some time to change the current unsafe behaviors.*

The team decided on an OSHA rate of 2.5%, which ended up being about seven injuries in a year. Considering we had over 45 injuries the previous year, this was still a lofty goal, but we took into account the improvements the team had made toward the end of the previous year.

The team believed that we had a great group of hourly team members (and I agreed) who were misunderstood and deserved better from the leadership team. For the past several years, the hourly team members received an incentive of only $.05 per hour worked every quarter in their paychecks even though they had the ability to earn $1.10. This was a great motivational program the company offered that gave hourly team members a "bonus" if the building did well in the areas of performance and quality, which involves taking care of our customers (the stores that sell the goods). At the end of the quarter, a team member on a high-performing team could earn $1.10 for every hour he/she worked, which adds up to little over $2,000 yearly. To many families, this is a huge deal. Instead, the team members on our team did not even pay attention to this perk because they were consistently considered low performing. The leaders decided to set a new goal at $.80 per hour. Again, another determined leader approached me questioning why the goal was not set to the maximum perk of $1.10, so I explained:

> We can build trust and credibility with the team members if we can establish enough discipline and process improvement to earn an $.80 incentive. The hourly team members will be astonished when they get that first bonus for the quarter that is $.75 per hour more than they were used to getting. This will show results that speak to them through their bank accounts. Remember, we do not want to be a one-hit wonder, we want to establish a foundation that can withstand the test of time.

Turnover was a problem having a huge impact on many industries and companies, not just ours. There were 10 other distribution centers within a 50-mile radius performing similar operations to my team. The unemployment rate was less than 3%. In the previous year, my building alone spent

~$1 million dollars on training hourly team members just to see them leave the company. This was a major issue impacting operational performance, safety, and culture. When I first arrived to lead the team, there were roughly 600 hourly employees on three shifts. After a quick analysis, I determined the team needed more than 750 hourly employees on four shifts to run a safer, smoother, more efficient operation. I never wanted to get the team back into the situation they were currently in, where team members worked 40 extra hours of overtime to accomplish the workload, so I set a goal of 850 hourly team members. Imagine hiring over 200 team members with a 35% turnover rate. This was not an easy task for our HR department, but they were troopers. They did an amazing job and accomplished this task. The leaders believed if we could retain the team members on the team and have a lower turnover rate, this would help to achieve many of the other goals such as performance.

Although we had several goals, I do want to highlight our rationale for development and team member engagement. The company provides a team member engagement budget to spend on the team for the year. Many teams within the company (including the previous leadership team) did not spend all the money in the budget on engagement, but instead used these funds to offset some of their financial performance shortcomings. This never made any sense to me. Here is a great program the company offers leaders to allow them to thank, recognize, and appreciate team members, and many distribution centers did not take advantage of it. The number one complaint of many team members about their senior leadership team in all distribution centers was, "My management team does not recognize my achievements." This was not going to be the case in our team. The goal was to spend 100% of the money on the recognition and appreciation of team members.

In addition, the path to a job in management was confusing. There were several hourly team members who aspired to be salaried leaders within the building. Now, I am a proponent of bringing in talent from the outside to give a different perspective, but I also believe in promoting from within as well. There were no solid development programs preparing a path to leadership for hourly team members, which is something I desperately wanted to change. The leaders set a goal of promoting five hourly team members to salaried positions. This did not have to mean a position within our building. Moreover, the leaders were adamant the standards of excellence would not be lowered to ensure we hit the goal.

PATHWAY TO ACHIEVE THE GOALS: SETTING INITIATIVES

In order for the team to realistically achieve all 10 goals, it was imperative to have initiatives the team worked on together. These initiatives helped move the business forward toward achieving the goals. The team created these 10 initiatives for the first year:

- Initiative 1: Parking Plan / Equipment Distribution Plan

- Initiative 2: Wrapper Production

- Initiative 3: Non-engineering Standard Production

- Initiative 4: Operation Purge

- Initiative 5: Customer Service Load Strap

- Initiative 6: Dry Racks to Conventional

- Initiative 7: Safety Fun Program Sequel

- Initiative 8: Turnover Reduction Initiative

- Initiative 9: Path to Leadership/Development to Lead/Area Leader High Potential

- Initiative 10: Value Added Team Building

I realize that these initiatives do not mean much to the reader since you were not there, but try to think about this when you are leading your own team. Is the initiative on your marketing team to be more efficient with brand planning for the following year? Is there a better way to track marketing spend within the market? Is there a better process in your finance department that would enable all teams in the company to manage their P&L and gather the right data needed to make decisions? Is there a better way to develop business cases? Are there initiatives within your procurement team that could improve supplier relations or onboard new vendors faster to the company? There are initiatives each team can work on throughout the year to make their team better.

Most likely because of my background in the military, I believe in the effectiveness of standards and discipline. I believe that if a team performs the standards set forth to 100% of their ability day in and day out, the team has the best chance of success. One of the most challenging goals my Eagles leaders set was the operational performance goal of 170 cases per hour (CPH). The team currently performed at 150 CPH and ranked at the bottom of the company for DCs. There were several reasons for the low performance; however, I wanted the leaders to focus on what they could control and to be intentional about the actions they took to make the team better. Four of the 10 initiatives were tied to performance and improving the team efficiency (performing the same workload with fewer labor hours). Many of these initiatives were bold; many other teams in the company would not dare to attempt them. I wanted the team to challenge the status quo. If we failed, there was an opportunity to learn, grow, and adjust the initiative or process.

The other initiatives were tailored to safety, quality, and customer service. For instance, safety is always considered something that is important but it seems dull and boring. Why couldn't we make safety fun? We could and we did. We started with a Standard Operating Procedure (I will cover the whole process of foundational development in another chapter) to explain the program and the intent behind it. The leaders involved all teams and shifts for a whole month and graded the engagement of the team members every day. The leaders walked around with candy and asked safety questions to individual team members. They caught team members performing safe acts similar to *Whale Done!* methodology and rewarded them with candy and a special "thank you".[4] Every week had a different theme.

For example, one week might be super hero week where team members were encouraged to dress up as their favorite superhero (I dressed up as Spiderman. I mean Spiderman is pretty awesome!). This program and its initiative were twofold; one, it put safety as the topic of conversation every day, and two, it showed the leaders which team members were engaged and which were not. The unengaged were not bad team members; the leader just needed to engage with them more by explaining the "why" behind our actions.

I truly wanted to create development programs that hourly team members and mid-level leaders could participate in and provide opportunities for them to grow professionally. Initiative nine became somewhat of an obsession of mine because it was critical to achieving long-term success for the team without me leading it. At this moment in time, there was no leadership bench. There were no hourly team members or mid-level leaders capable of stepping up into a higher role without the team suffering an impact in performance and a setback in the vision. There were programs within the company that other buildings approved for their leadership development programs, but they were not good. The programs did not make leaders, encourage others to grow or learn, and they were not effective. The programs lasted a year with no selection process or accountability for day-to-day and/or in-class levels of engagement. Chapter 7 is dedicated to explaining the proper way to create great leadership development programs.

At the end of the seven-hour vision and goal setting session, the Eagles team became laser focused on the year. I explained to everyone at the end of the meeting:

> *The vision we created—to provide a safe, results-driven atmosphere, built upon integrity, teamwork, and professionalism—is what each of us leaders will use to make decisions in the future. If we are engaged in an activity that does not help us achieve the goals we set forth, then we should not be focused on it. Each one of you has ownership of and accountability for achieving the ini-*

tiatives, and every meeting we have, every conversation we engage in, will center around our vision and how we plan to accomplish our goals.

Vision and goal setting is not just about the meeting. The meeting was the easy part; the difficult challenge was the journey to get everyone to buy into them. It was going to require discipline to stay the course. There are always difficult times, resistance, and anchor draggers (individuals dedicated to inhibiting momentum and progress). As long as you have the best interest of the team at heart, there will always be significantly more people on the team who want to see the team succeed than those who don't. The rest of the chapters support the vision and how to make it stick, but everything starts with the establishment of the vision. A clear vision, along with the courage to follow through, dramatically increases your chances of coming to the end of the year, looking back with deep satisfaction, and thinking, "We DID it! We succeeded. We finished. This year MATTERED."

KEY TAKEAWAYS OF CHAPTER 4:

In Chapter 4, I broke down ways to develop a vision and set meaningful goals.

1. Everyone must believe in the vision in order for the vision to be the milieu in which decisions are made.

2. A vision acts as the North Star to keep the team headed in the right direction when outside elements knock the team off course.

3. Just writing a vision on a wall and talking about it at the beginning of the year does not mean the vision is alive. If only 50% of your team understands the vision, the team will never achieve its goals.

4. Goals should be SMART and should allow the team to move toward achieving the vision.

5. Initiatives should be defined, clearly articulated, and set up to help the team achieve their desired goals.

6. Creating a vision is the easier part. Having the discipline to keep the vision front and center of all decisions day in and day out is the hard part.

CHAPTER FIVE:

STRUCTURE & ORGANIZATION

"Structure and discipline give us freedom."

~ Andy Fox

THERE IS A NICE book written by Admiral William H. McRaven called *Make Your Bed: Little Things Can Change Your Life...and Maybe the World* that uses the practice of making one's bed every morning to prove the point that little things can make a huge impact on a person's life. Sometimes we make business harder than it has to be by shooting from the hip or diving right in before thinking through how things should be done. Admiral McRaven talks about having the discipline every morning to make the bed; a simple task that takes two minutes, and which can set the tone for the rest of the day.

Many people are "checklist" people, and most people would admit they feel great when they accomplish things on their list throughout the day. When a person completes an item on the list, dopamine is released in the brain. Dopamine is a naturally produced neurotransmitter that acts like a drug. According to WebMD, dopamine plays a role in how we feel pleasure. It's a big part of our unique human ability to think and plan. It helps us strive, focus, and find things interesting.[1]

According to dietitian and nutrition expert, Erica Julson, "When dopamine is released in large amounts, it creates feelings of pleasure and reward, which motivates you to repeat a specific behavior."[2] By starting with a simple task in the morning, you start to build momentum for the remainder of the day because you want to repeat the pleasure you received from making your bed and completing that first task. You instill structure into your life. It is no surprise this simple concept came from a military leader like Admiral McRaven. The military is a very structured organization that teaches standards and disciplines. It is difficult to have structure and organizational skills without having discipline; they go hand-in-hand.

Once a leader establishes or starts to establish trust and credibility, evaluating the current structures in place is important. If there is no structure within the team, it will be difficult to build a sustainable culture because it will crumble at the first sign of challenges and/or failure. And mark my words: there will be challenges and failures. No team can escape this, which is not a bad thing. As Michael Jordan once said, "I've missed more than 9,000 shots in my career. I've lost almost 300 games. Twenty-six times I've been trusted to take the game winning shot and missed. I've failed over and over and over again in my life. And that is why I succeed."[3] Failures are not a bad thing, but you need to use those failures as opportunities to learn, grow, and adjust. Do not waste a failure moment.

Developing a vision and setting goals is the first step in establishing structure within a team, as discussed in the previous Chapter. Vision and goal setting is all about clarity and ensuring everyone understands the North Star concept and where the team is going. Being organized in a thoughtful way and establishing structure within a team provides this clarity.

BUILDING MOMENTUM: STANDARD OPERATING PROCEDURES (SOPs)
What do I mean by structure and organization? I did not know it when I was in the trenches with my teams, but the academic world calls this organizational structure. Will Kenton with Investopedia says, "An orga-

nizational structure is a system that outlines how certain activities are directed in order to achieve the goals of an organization. These activities can include rules, roles, and responsibilities. The organizational structure also determines how information flows between levels within the company. Having an organizational structure in place allows companies to remain efficient and focused."[4]

The military is the best example when it comes to organizational structure. There is a rank structure; every soldier, enlisted person, and officer knows and understands his/her role and responsibilities. There are Standard Operating Procedures (SOP) that outline everything you could possibly need to know. If you want to know how to prepare for and pass a vehicle inspection, there is an SOP for it. If you want to know how to fly a UH-60 Blackhawk helicopter, there is a manual and SOP that will tell you. If you want to know how to lead a Company as a Company Commander, there is an SOP. SOPs act as guidelines that, if followed, will set you and the team up for success. SOPs adjust and change over time as the military evolves within its environment. The SOPs are based on the experiences of other servicemen and women who gained the knowledge in the past in order to establish a one consistent way mindset. Considering the fact the United States Military is a finely tuned machine that protects our freedom, this is probably something worth paying attention to, if not adopting. Yet, when you look at some businesses today, there is a lack of structure and organization. If you look at your own company today, and you have two people doing the same job differently, or two departments operating completely differently from one another, then there is no clarity around which organizational structure to follow. This might work in the short-term, but this could lead to stagnation and falling below legitimate standards because no one truly knows what the best way looks like. All they know is the way they conducted the job in the past or the standard in which was taught to them by someone else, which might not be most efficient.

APPLICATION: THE EAGLES

Within the first three months of joining the Eagles team, I observed, listened, met with the leaders and team members, and wrote a lot of notes. I recorded in my notebook anything I observed that involved safety, quality, performance, development, leadership, and efficiency including great things the team did, questions I had about processes, questionable decisions, the effectiveness of meetings, and who the "go-to" hourly team members were, among other things. At the end of each day, I typed my notes into a master Word document. I ended up with eight pages of notes and a lot of work to do. One thing I quickly realized was this team was not as broken as the executives within the company leadership team believed. It was bent, but certainly not broken; there were good leaders and hourly team members who came to work every day wanting to make a difference.

I took another three weeks to pull together themes from my notes and prioritize the areas the leadership team needed to focus on immediately. In the next Chapter I will discuss how I put it all together. What stuck out like a sore thumb was the need to improve the discipline of the team members and the structure within the team. The company did a great job of establishing Standard Operating Procedures on how to run a store, how to do a job, and how to operate in a distribution center. The problem was there were thousands of team members and each building operated differently. In addition, there were over 10,000 Standard Operating Procedures. You can see how the various teams might interpret SOPs differently.

The prevailing mindset in many companies is, "We have always done it this way. I will teach the next person the same way I was taught." The issue with this mindset is if the beginning person was taught the process incorrectly, then it trickles through teams the wrong way. In addition, the business is always changing, so teams need to adjust and be flexible. Teaching the same wrong way every time does not allow the business to be flexible through the changes in the business.

I originally had three different shifts, two on weekdays (morning and evening), and one on weekends. The first shift was operating under a different structure than the second shift, and the third shift was not following any standards or processes. Every leader thought his/her way was the best and none of it aligned to company standards. The individual leaders and teams were inconsistent. They were inconsistent with their processes, how they held team members accountable, how they provided vacation time, how they planned their day, how they led, and how they recognized team members. In fact, none of the leaders recognized their team members, so I suppose this was consistent, but not in a good way. The Senior Leaders essentially reacted like firefighters putting out fires and solving problems as they came up all day long. The mid-level leaders could not leave the operations desk because they had to ensure the work for the day finished. And the hourly team members went as fast or slow as they wanted without any understanding of their jobs, purpose, or roles within the team and the company.

Given my military and personal background, I had an obsession with order and structure. I believed–and still to this day believe–that standards and discipline hold the keys to freedom and success. I knew during this time period that in order to build this team the right way, I must establish structure and organization within the team despite the fact every leader and hourly team member was comfortable just "getting through the day" their own way.

WORKING STRATEGY: FOUR STAGES OF TEAM DEVELOPMENT

Like any group trying to be a high-performing team, we had to follow the Four Stages of Team Development (Forming, Storming, Norming, and Performing) closely. Now, if you have never studied the Four Stages of Team Development as defined by psychologist Bruce Tuckman, I am going to walk you through the definitions, show how these stages applied to the team, and demonstrate how important it is to understand the stages. I am talking about this now because imposing structure and organization was crucial to get the team back on track, and this happens to be a critical component to the first stage of team development. If this concept interests you, I urge you to dive deeper into other books about this topic.

Four Stages of Team Development[5]

1. *Forming:*

Group tends to emphasize procedural matters. Group inter-action is very tentative and polite. Leader dominates the deci-sion-making process and plays a very important role in moving the group forward.

2. *Storming:*

Conflict between members and between members and lead-ers are characteristics of this stage. Members question authority as it relates to the group objectives, structure, and procedures. Groups resist the attempts of their leaders to move them toward independence. Members try to define their roles in the group.

3. *Norming:*

Group begins to take responsibility and ownership of its goals, procedures, and behaviors. The focus is on working together ef-ficiently. Group norms are enforced on the group by the group itself.

4. *Performing:*

Members have a sense of pride in the group, its accomplish-ments, and their role in the group. Members are confident in their ability to contribute to the group and feel free to ask for or give assistance.

DEVELOPMENT 101: HOW TO ESTABLISH STRUCTURE

At the start of team development, every shift operated the way they want-ed to operate. Every leader utilized the processes they believed were cor-rect, and the leaders reacted to every problem until another problem came along. The other team members just tried to "make it through the day."

And although the organization had thousands of Standard Operating Procedures, not many of them were being followed. The first step I established was a Back-to-Basics Standard Operating Procedure. My belief was that if we could not do the little things right on a daily basis, we would never be able to execute complex problems and situations. When big issues occurred, the team freaked out under pressure and failed to execute the operation efficiently. This approach led to poor safety, poor quality, poor performance, poor engagement, and poor decisions. It was imperative to get everyone in the building on the same page. Every team member had to be rowing the boat in the same rhythm to go in the direction we wanted to go. This started a three-month initiative to develop the Back-to-Basics Standard Operating Procedure.

BACK-TO-BASICS STANDARD OPERATING PROCEDURE EXAMPLE

Below is an excerpt from the Back-to-Basics SOP to exhibit the level of detail placed in these documents. There was a level of information that provided clarity, but enough room for the leaders and team members to be independent to grow and make his/her own decisions:

> **PURPOSE:** The purpose of this document is to lay out the performance day-to-day activities for the team leaders. It is extremely important for all shifts and teams to be on the same page, and for all leaders in the building to be consistent in what they do. This document is the foundation upon which the Eagles built their vision (Provide a safe, results-driven atmosphere built upon integrity, teamwork, and professionalism). If a leader will follow the below expectations, they will meet the standard of the team. This does not mean they are a High Potential Leader; it simply means they met the status quo. The document is not all encompassing; it is a living document that can be changed at any point in order to meet the changing demands of the business. This SOP is the foundation from which everything in our business stems. It provides the basic elements (blocking and tackling) of the business.

This document walked every team member who read it through the "day in the life of an Eagle Leader." It explained what a typical day from start to finish should look like for a mid-level leader who interacted daily with the hourly team members. As it says in the Purpose section, this document was "living"; it had the ability to change as the business demanded. In three years, this foundational document was adjusted three times to be better, more clear, and more effective for all involved. It explained what a leader should do to prepare the team for success before the operation, how to maintain order and control during the operation, how to recognize team members throughout the year, how to ensure team members complied to the standards set forth, and how to conduct a proper handoff to the team working after them. The document is granular and very detailed, but allows enough leeway (guardrails) for the leaders to operate with authority and empowerment.

Below are the main elements of the Back-to-Basics SOP used for the distribution center environment, but which could easily be adapted for many other types of business teams to establish structure.

- Shift-to-shift handoff

- Start of the week administration duties

- Tactical planning– plan your day ahead of time

- Start-up meetings

- The operation

  - Lean six sigma mentality

  - Praise and holding the standard

  - Spend time with the team members on the floor, in their environment

- End of shift closeout

- End of shift administration duties

- Consistency walks– does the environment look better than it did when you received it?

- Accountability standards

- Performance standards

In the Appendix of this document, there were examples and tools for leaders to follow. This document listed the most critical components for establishing structure during the Forming Stage. As the definition states, the decision-making responsibility rests heavily on the shoulders of the leader of the team (me, in this instance) at this stage. It is important to note this is a temporary situation, and as more leaders see the importance of imposing a consistent structure and organization, they will buy into the process and start to make decisions themselves.

You might ask, "How did you develop this document? Did you write it all by yourself?" I do not suggest creating an SOP document by yourself and trying to roll it out to a team because it will not stick very well in that scenario. I was ultimately the person who put the document together, but I included the leaders in the conversations throughout the process. I did not make up new rules. I leveraged policies and procedures the company already established in its 1,000 other SOPs, but consolidated them into an easy-to-interpret document that made sense for our team, given their state of development. In addition, I asked leaders to read it and provide input. Hourly team members validated the information contained therein. And most importantly, I rolled it out the proper way.

THE PROPER WAY: ROLLING OUT AN SOP
The rollout of any document, program, test, guidance, or directive is where I saw many leaders and teams fail in the military, as well as in business. The biggest problem organizations face is not everyone is on the same page in terms of standards and expectations. When a process or program is initiated, it often never reaches the team members actually executing the program. This is due to a lack of communication from the leaders within a

team. Leaders fail during this process because they do not give enough attention to properly passing the information along. Leaders assume everyone on the team will read the email or letter and fully adopt whatever the leader says. This works great in fairytales, but it is not the case in the real world.

How a Standard Operating Procedure or program is rolled out should be just as detailed as the program itself. I developed an actual Standard Operating Procedure on how to properly roll out programs because, prior to this, my leaders were just reading documents to team members during the beginning of the day "start-up" meetings. The problem with this approach is when anyone gives a presentation or a speech to a group of individuals, the listeners only retain 10% of what they hear.[6] As a result, you cannot develop a plan or program by talking about it one time. As I am sure you might have read, it takes ~21 days to change a behavior and normally when a team rolls out an SOP, it is because they want to change something.

Every document developed to express a fundamental element of the business is written at a basic level, so that everyone can quickly grasp the purpose and intent behind the document. The documents do not work unless a team has great leaders who understand the vision and goals, believe in the process, and are committed to execution and results. Every team must know what makes them successful, because when the 'wheels come off' the operation/business (and they will), the team must know how to get the operation back on track with minimal cost to the company in time or money.

TAKE THE NECESSARY TIME: PROPER STEPS TO A ROLLOUT

1. The document is written by the Senior Leader on the team with input from other leaders on the team at all different levels of command. Remember, when establishing structure and organization, it is in the Forming Stage, so direction and drive comes from the senior leader.

2. After the document is written, it is given to between three and five different leaders to review and make corrections. At least two of the leaders conducting the review should not be involved directly in the execution. The purpose of this is to ensure simplicity and ease of understanding. The author should not have to explain in more detail for the reader to figure it out. I always say, "Give it to a seven-year-old. If he/she can figure it out, then it must be pretty simple and clear."

3. Following corrections and feedback, the document is briefed in an All Leader Meeting to ensure that all leaders know and understand the purpose and intent behind the new document. It also gives everyone a chance to ask questions. If you cannot answer the "why" questions, then perhaps you should not be implementing the change. The accountability levels for failing to adhere to the standard are clearly defined. This is not meant to be threatening:

> a. Many companies today talk about "accountability" as being instrumental to their success, yet most employees of that company do not know what they are actually held accountable to because it has not been clearly defined.

> b. The U.S. military is the largest organization in the world. Soldiers are all clearly informed of their left and right limits (guardrails); they know what they can and cannot do. The Rules of Engagement (ROE) are clearly defined. Sure, there are some gray areas, but the soldiers understand that if they do not follow the ROE, they could be removed from their post, discharged altogether, or in serious cases, even go to prison. So why do the CEOs of Fortune 500 companies not think it makes sense to clearly tell leaders what the accountability and consequences are for not meeting standards?

c. Brené Brown has a great saying that I think fits well with accountability and structure: "Clear is kind. Unclear is unkind."[7]

4. Each leader has three to five weeks to effectively communicate the new document to the next level team members in a small group setting. This three-to-five weeks is negotiable depending how big of a change it is.

5. All leaders should communicate a "Go-Live" date for the team to adjust to the change. This date should be the same for the whole team. The "Go-Live" date should be the date in which accountability begins and all team members should comply with the new standard.

a. This is a step that many leaders miss because they just assume that once a plan/program is communicated, everyone is bought in, understands everything about it, and will follow it to a T. This is not true. Depending on the behavior you are trying to change, a team member might have performed the behavior for several years; they cannot just switch that behavior because the leaders said so. That is unrealistic.

b. Give the leaders and team members enough time to adjust. Consider it a grace period or a learning period during which anyone can ask questions. The leaders must understand the "why" because if you cannot explain the "why" very simply, then you probably should not be making the change to begin with. I mention this a second time because it is that important.

6. The document should be emailed to all of the leaders on the team so they can reference it whenever they need to.

Leaders always ask, "Is there something in the document that the other teammates should not see?" The answer is no; you should not write something you would not want every team member to read. This is how a divide between "us" and "them," "management" and "hourly" is created. Transparency is critical to trust and credibility, which (remember) is the foundation of leadership.

7. The Senior Leaders within the team inspect what they expect by checking to ensure the new program was executed properly and followed accordingly.

> a. This ties very closely to Step 5b; if it is truly important, the Senior Leaders will go into their team members' environments and interact with them. Ask everyone questions. Spot-check to see if they fully understand it. Ask them questions to determine what they do not understand. If you have multiple shifts on your team, you have to talk to all team members on all shifts. If you have support staff, they should be just as "read in" as everyone else.

> b. Lead from the front. Catch team members doing the right things and praise them for it publicly (unless this team member does not like public recognition). Do not just catch people messing up. If you have never read *Whale Done*,[8] this is a great book that describes the importance of catching people doing good. Make sure your teammates see you adhering to the same program you asked them to buy into. Imagine if they catch you, as the leader, not following the program. Credibility is shot; gone, start over. You, as the leader, always have eyes on you even when you think you do not.

8. Lastly, you cannot just set it and leave it. A growing team is like a plant; you have to continue to water the plant in order for it to grow roots and thrive. This program should be like a plant you added to your greenhouse. It takes constant support. Talk about it in meetings. Explain to leaders and team members how it fits into the overall vision for the team.

After you roll out a program, SOP, or new information, empowerment of your leaders and team members helps maintain it and keep it relevant as your team grows in other areas. Each document is written to provide the leader with a standard by which to operate the business. It is structured and detailed for the "perfect environment," which is not realistic because things can and will go wrong in business. There are times the business will not allow for the SOPs to be followed exactly as written. The leaders have the freedom to make a decision on what aspects of the SOP will be followed and which to ignore for the day based on obstacles faced and situations encountered. The leader is empowered to make the best decision for the team as it relates to the vision. The SOPs should act as a 'rubber band' which may be stretched enough from its original intent to meet the demands of the business, but then contracts back to its original form once the business is back to normal. This is a difficult part of executing the SOPs because it is human nature to go back to the "old way" things were, even if it is not the right way. We know it is not the right way because the leader would not have changed it if it had been the one consistent way possible at the time of creation. The most dangerous phrases in the English language are, "We have always done it that way" or "We used to do it that way." This way of thinking only results in stagnation and failure.

A well-structured and well-organized team will be successful in good times and bad. They can weather any storm and perform under any conditions. By following an organized and structured Playbook, as I called it, the team will effectively communicate to the leaders and team members in order to build a connection, which will ultimately lead to commitment from all members of the team. The end state is that no matter who the leader is, the foundation/structure remains the same and the execution remains the same. High expectations mean a high level of success and success is defined by meeting the team's true potential.[9]

CREATING A BLUEPRINT: THE PLAYBOOK

The Back-to-Basics SOP was the first SOP written exclusively for this team and it truly established the foundation for the team to build from. As the Eagles team progressed, this document evolved; I compared this document to the Bill of Rights, which are the first 10 amendments in the U.S. Constitution. As with the Constitution of the United States, the Bill of Rights established the foundation by which the rest of the country would be built.

The remaining documents written stemmed from and always reinforced the Back-to-Basics SOP, like amendments in the Constitution. These documents made up the Playbook. The Playbook was how I planned to establish organizational structure within the team. I established a comprehensive one consistent way of doing things. I knew I had to mimic the military, take all the experiences of those doing it right within the company, and put in place what made sense for the team I was leading. In the next Chapter I will discuss how I put it all together using the analogy of a jigsaw puzzle, but for now I want to discuss some of the elements that made up the Playbook. Remember, the team collaborated to determine what the vision would be:

> *Provide a safe, results-driven atmosphere built upon integrity, teamwork, and professionalism*

The different SOPs within the Playbook all had a similar structure for consistency and were created to advance the team toward the vision.

PLAY-BY-PLAY: PEAK SEASON OPERATIONS SOPS

As the Back-to-Basics SOP was rolled out, there were several other important documents that would be critical to the progression of the team and reinforcement of the Back-to-Basics SOP. As the team entered the Forming Stage, where structure was added to the day-to-day activities, I wanted to make it a big deal. The team was several months into the implementation of structure with the Back-to-Basics SOP when we entered the biggest peak season for the company.

I mentioned in Chapter 2, peak seasons are based on holidays and high volume, high labor time periods. Thanksgiving is one of the biggest times of the year for sales in grocery distribution centers because so many people have family dinners. Success for a distribution center is determined by whether or not the team is able to keep the shelves stocked as customers flood the stores. If trucks are late to the different stores, then there is not enough time to ensure the shelves are stocked and full. This is bad for business. I am sure many of you have experienced an empty grocery store at some point in your life and were frustrated because the store did not have something you needed or wanted. It is not a good experience.

Also in Chapter 2, I mentioned prior to my arrival, the Eagles failed a lot of stores and made a lot of mistakes that caused the level of service to severely decrease and caused the team to lose a lot of credibility with the stores we serviced. This was prior to any structure; this was prior to entering the Forming Stage. I used SOPs to help structure guidance given to the team during these peak seasons. Every peak season SOP had a specific name associated with it and I referred to them as operations because of my background in the military. In the military, it is called an Operations Order (OPORD) and encompasses Situation, Mission, Execution, Service and Support, and finally, Command and Signal. These are the five paragraphs that make up an OPORD. In simple terms, this is how commanders communicate simple and complex plans/missions to their teams.

For example, if I were flying a combat air assault mission, I would bring my aircrew and team together. I would explain the **Situation**: There is a High Value Target (HVT) in a village at Point X who is planning to attack a town if we do not secure it. **Mission**: The mission is to fly the Special Forces team from Point X to Point Y at 2300 hours on a specific date. **Execution:**

I would explain in detail the route to fly, expectations along the route, enemy situation, and contingencies. Everything that a team member needs to know about the operation is in this section. **Service & Support**: I would explain refueling expectations, where to get food, rest, or utilize artillery support for the mission. **Command & Signal**: Communication is a key element to any operation, so it is imperative to be clear how, what radios will be used, what frequency, and who in the chain of command for the mission makes the critical decisions. I named the Air Mission Commander, Ground Force Commander, or Pilot in Command for each aircraft. By the time I briefed the mission, everyone knew his/her role and responsibilities. There might be a few questions, but they were mostly for clarification.

I wanted this level of detail for our critical time periods such as peak seasons. I named this particular peak season for Thanksgiving Operation *Turkey Assault*. This document, along with all the others to follow always started with a Purpose. It was critical for every team member to understand the importance of the document. I used operational names, similar to those used in the military because that made it easy to reference, and naming an event makes it real, tangible, and physical. These were the sections of the document that described in detail how the execution should occur:

1. **Purpose**: What is the reason for reading the document in the first place? Bottom Line, Up Front (BLUF)

2. **Intent**: Why are we communicating this? Why are we doing this? Why does it matter?

3. **Team Start-Up Communication Methods**: This is how the plan was to be rolled out to every team member on every shift, and the reporting methods to be used.

4. **Detailed Schedule**: This explained the schedule for all shifts because they were different from normal operations and all team members needed to be aware of other shifts in case they needed to help out on a different schedule.

5. **Changes**: This highlighted any changes to normal operations worth noting.

6. **Maintenance**: The maintenance team played a critical role during peak season and could make or break the team if they were not on the ball. It explained their hours of operation, priorities of work, and expectations during the peak season.

7. **Equipment Breakdown**: This was part of the planning to ascertain if there was enough equipment to ensure success. This enabled the team to determine if we needed to rent or bring in other equipment from another building.

8. **Overtime Plan**: This becomes a necessity (at times) during peak season, so this allowed us to control the labor and have control over who was in the building for accountability purposes (know who and where your teammates are).

9. **Contingency Plans**: Murphy's Law ("Anything that can go wrong, will go wrong") will prevail in times of stress; it always does. It's better to plan for it. This laid out potential problem situations that could occur or had occurred in the past on this team or on other teams elsewhere in the company.

10. **Tasks to Team Members**: All the leaders had their names on the document which also listed the expectations for each of them.

11. **End State**: At the end of the operation, what did success look like? Success for one team might be different for another, but defining success is key to that success.

12. **After Action Review**: There would be a time after the operation to reflect on what went well and what the team needed to improve upon, so adjustments could be made to the upcoming peak season or to this peak season in the following year.

After I wrote the document, I shared it with several leaders to get their input for changes. Once the document had reached a place where everyone could understand it, I leveraged an All Leader Meeting to brief the document in PowerPoint format. I had team members back brief the plan to me and had them brief team members at all levels. The "Back Brief" is a key element to any plan. So many times the leader will brief a plan and assume everyone understands it. If the leader asks, he/she will get several nodding heads because no one wants to ask a question that prolongs the meeting. Calling on someone to back brief the plan is a way to check understanding. Because no one will understand the plan as well as the leader who planned it, it is just as critical to success to have the listeners explain it back since they will be the ones executing it. A leader cannot just brief the team and then walk away. He/she must act as the CEO–Chief Execution Officer.[10] I would love to say I came up with that, but I learned that from Dave Ramsey and Patrick Lencioni. I spot-checked teams to ensure they understood the expectations and asked team members again several days prior to the peak season to ensure they understood the plan. This Operation Turkey Assault document reinforced the Back-to-Basics SOP and built on the momentum. You will notice how I followed the same rollout process discussed earlier.

The team flawlessly executed the plan. Small hiccups and challenges occurred, but not one leader succumbed to the pressure. They had a plan they felt comfortable with and everyone did his/her job. A few days after Thanksgiving, the team came together for an after action review to determine the sustains and improvements of the operational peak season. I wrote notes and put it in a formal document. I sent this to all team members to review. I used this document to make adjustments to the next peak season. In addition, I sent the AAR to my peers in other buildings within the company for them to learn from and make adjustments as they felt worked for their team. There was an Operations Order (OPORD) with a name for every peak season that occurred for the remainder of the year and for the years to follow. This all became part of the Playbook; a one stop shop for all SOPs and guidance as to how the Eagles team operated.

The team was now fully into the Forming Stage and began to shift into the Storming Stage, where those who were resistant became vocal. The team encountered a serious stage that could have derailed everything, if it were not for the work we had done in establishing the structure of the team in the Forming Stage.

BLESSING IN DISGUISE: LETTER AND ROLL INTO PIVOT POINT

The operational charts showed a steady incline in safety, quality, performance, and engagement over a month's time period as the team members began to buy in and build momentum. The executive leaders within the highest levels at the organization could not understand how this distribution center improved and transformed so quickly. They thought Standard Operating Procedures and the emphasis on structure were silly and an unproductive waste of time.

Executive Leader to me: "Patrick, the culture here is all about taking care of the people. Your method is quirky and off-culture."

My response: "Providing structure and clarity IS taking care of people. I am focusing on the 90% of the team members who care about the team and the company's success. I am not catering to the 10% who want to keep the 'Good Ol' Boy System' and want everything back the way it was, which, by the way, landed the building at the bottom in terms of engagement, safety, and performance."

One Friday, I had left work a bit early to go spend time with my family when I got a call to return to the building right away. I was told to check my email; I opened a letter from a team member in my building to the corporate headquarters stating that I, Patrick Hall, was destroying the culture and that a union was beginning to form. The organization believes that unions would destroy the company, and I totally agree. I truly respect the company for their views on unions because I believe unions are for teams that do not have leaders who listen to their employees and team members. The email was dated back almost two months when I saw it; apparently, it had gotten lost in a corporate transition.

The executive leadership team believed they were behind the curve because of the date of the letter. When the team member sent the letter, the team was in the middle of the Forming Stage, which can be difficult for team members resistant to change because there is a lot happening and a whole new structure is put in place. Since then, the results began to show in the performance and engagement of the team. The engagement was most important because leaders and teammates expressed how proud they were of the progress of the team.

Before I begin this next section, it is important to note that I take full ownership of what happened. It was evident that while I thought I was clear on the direction of the team, I was not. Whatever positive progress the team made halted immediately. The company senior leaders brought in a team of 10 corporate managers to assess the seriousness of the letter. A Senior Vice President stood in front of my 800 employees in a General Meeting to explain the letter and apologize to them for what I had done. She cast the blame on me and said the executive leadership team is involved now to fix the issue. I looked at the faces of the team members. They had no idea what she was talking about. Without asking me any questions, without doing any investigation, and without any warning, the VP single-handedly delayed our progress by months. She was not involved in the conversation about how to turn the team culture around. She could not understand why I would write an SOP laying out specific standards when the company already had that in place and stated that every team/building should be operated the same way.

This was extremely embarrassing and to overcome this shame, I took a look at myself to see what I could have done differently in my process. I did not point blame. I took ownership of the state of the team. I slowed the process down, but I did not change the course of what I believed needed to happen to get us on the right path. I believe the VP did what she thought was right at the moment. She thought she had to take immediate action to address the feelings of some of the team members. It was an extremely tough and trying time in my life, but it made me stronger as a leader. I adjusted course, but I did not change the trajectory of the team. I truly believed (and still do) in the team-building process and knew in my heart the team was much further into the journey than the letter revealed. These re-evaluations and adjustments were necessary for the team to end where we did three years later. It was also an amazing lesson I learned on how not to lead. I learned from the VP not to react without gathering at least some of the facts and both sides of a story. I learned to not jump to a conclusion on something I am not well versed in, but to ask questions to educate myself. It showed me how to handle big moments of uncertainty and to take a step back and gather the facts before casting judgment.

Not only did the VP's response to the letter undermine my authority, but also, the leaders lost faith that they could achieve the high expectations being asked of them. It is my belief that a leader's job is to unlock the true potential of those he/she serves. It is not in the best interest of the team to set easy goals that can be achieved within a week and expect to move the business / team forward. My failure was trying to control too much within the team. I checked in on 12 direct reports by checking on their five direct reports, which means I was verifying that all 50-plus leaders were held to the same standard. This is time consuming and I took my eyes off the strategy/vision and did not see the icebergs ahead of the team. The iceberg was that some leaders and team members were not as far along in the journey as I thought, which allowed their fear of the unknown to get the best of them.

The actions of the VP empowered the 10% of the team who wanted things to stay the way they were, and frustrated the 90% who were beginning to understand the direction and importance of the vision. For a month, the corporate team pulled team members off the operation floor, interviewed them and the leaders, and asked a bunch of questions. The team put all the comments into a large Microsoft Excel file and presented it to me and my boss. There was no evidence of a Union forming. There were only normal comments about a team trying to get better and navigate the four stages of team development. The damage was done, but there was a right way to look at the situation and a wrong way. The right way was to see the opportunity to build the momentum again and provide more clarity and leadership to the team.

Around this time, I was reading a book on pivoting from negative situations called *Switch: How to Change Things When Change is Hard*[11], which involved picking a point in time, and pivoting directly from that point to make things better. The message was: "Do not try to fix the past." As a result, I started gathering data points, looking at myself, and talking to the leaders and team members. The team was fully into the Storming Phase by now. I decided to develop a Standard Operating Procedure to get us back on track and called it Operation Pivot Point.

NEGOTIATING THE CROSSROAD: OPERATION PIVOT POINT

The leaders committed to the vision and goals were devastated by the impact the letter caused. I wanted the team to look to the future and forget about the past. I told them, "The past reminds you, but it does not define you." I decided to put together a presentation for the team in an All Leader Meeting. I started with the past and all of the great things the team implemented in the interim. By this time, the team had taken a Lean Six Sigma mentality approach to the operation. They began practicing Kaizen, which is the Japanese word for continuous improvement. The team measured Direct and Indirect Hours impacting the operational efficiencies on a daily/weekly/monthly basis, and began to see the big picture. Many of the leaders understood the proper utilization of labor hours from a business standpoint.

Every All Leader Meeting was set up the same way. An hourly team member was empowered to run the operation while every leader in the building attended the two-to-three-hour meeting. There was always food provided for lunch and a PowerPoint presentation prepared for them. For this particular meeting, the slides showed a chart of the team performance from the year prior. Then, the chart showed their significant improvement up until the time the letter and the corporate team entered the building–the chart dropped significantly like a stock market crash.

Many of the leaders struggled to understand how the team could get back on track after such a derailment. I spent 15 minutes recapping the past year and how the team made the improvements to safety, quality, performance, and engagement as a group. Then, I put up a slide showing where we were at that point:

I told the team:

> *We are at a crossroads right now. We can go back to the 'good old boy' system where mediocrity was accepted, or we can choose the tougher path. We can pivot right here, right now and gain back the momentum we experienced as a team over the past year. I propose we choose to engage in Operation Pivot Point.*

The next slide I put up was the Vision we developed as a team. I said,

> *No matter what happens next, our vision is what will get us back on track and enable us to move forward. It is our North Star!*

This occurred near the end of the year, so I felt the best time to activate Operation Pivot Point was at the start of the next year. This gave the team plenty of time to get back to the basics and follow the Playbook with the Standard Operating Procedures currently in place.

John Maxwell writes about "The Big Mo" in *The 21 Irrefutable Laws of Leadership*[12]. He points out that momentum is a critical element to any team's success. In the All Leader Meeting, I used the stock market chart to explain about the momentum the team created. The SOPs, standards and disciplines, performance tracking of Indirect and Utilization all helped create the momentum that enabled the improvements in safety, operational efficiencies, quality service to our customer, and morale of the team members.

I reminded them:

> *Momentum is important: Why do coaches in sports games call a time-out when the other team has everything going well and their own team cannot do anything right? Because it interrupts the other team's momentum. Momentum is easier to keep going than it is to start from scratch. If you are not a sports fan, then imagine riding a bike. When you ride a bike, it's much easier on your legs to steer and ride no-handed when you are already in motion, but when you come to a complete stop and start going again, it takes a lot more effort. Motivation and vision are key factors in developing momentum. We, as leaders cannot lose our passion and enthusiasm. One way to get past an interruption in the momentum is to honor and appreciate those who move the ball/business forward. Praise their efforts and reward their accomplishments–let's start with that.*

I realized it would not be as simple as getting everyone fired up in a meeting. That only lasts a short time. By the time Operation Pivot Point kicked off, the leaders acquired many "momentum tools" to help get us back on track. The leaders established team names in order to build team cohesion. Prior to the journey, there was no such thing as the Eagles—it was DC 1234. The traditional way of naming teams in the company was by function: "First Shift Dry Shipping, Second Shift Freezer Receiving, or Weekend Meat and Produce Shipping." These are not exactly names that motivate members to rally around. The Eagles created over 18 different team names, each with its own logo and brand personality: names such as Warriors, Smokin' Aces, Horsemen, Regulators, Gladiators, DawgPound, and Ghost Riders, to list a few. The building and hallways made these logos visible all over the place. There was even a performance-tracking board to show where each team ranked among the rest of the DC teams in the company. Some leaders might argue a performance tracking board encourages teams to be focused on the numbers only. I found that team members want to understand how they stack up against others. It also shows improvements. I used to have team members walk into my office and say, "Patrick, did you see the Warriors performance last week? We improved by three spots."

The company did something really great for its team members: each leader had a set annual employee relations budget to spend on each team member. In most buildings within the company, the budget was controlled by the senior leader in the building. I did not follow this practice; instead, my team member engagement budget was distributed to and managed by each of the leaders who were able to spend the funds on their own team for whatever made sense for them. There was an SOP written that set forth guidelines in order to keep everyone on the same page and ensure policy was still followed, but the leaders used this budget to truly appreciate their team members and reward them for doing great things.

Lastly, Operation Pivot Point was used to move leaders around. Some leaders were great and meshed well with other leaders and some did not. This was a critical time, and it was important to get the "right" people on the bus (as Jim Collins would say) AND to make sure that the right people were in the right spots on the bus. I explained the leadership moves to the team and, most importantly, the "why" behind the moves. I used data to back much of my reasoning. Then, on the first day of the company year, Operation Pivot Point kicked off.

The tone was set and the leaders responded. The team hit the ground running and picked up where they left off prior to the momentum interruption caused by the letter. The leaders inspected what they expected, safety within the building resumed with over 70 days without a medical injury, and the operational performance metrics continued to improve. The standards and disciplines were in place, and the team truly cared about achieving the vision and goals. The team brought on new talent at the hourly team member leader levels. Because of the structure in place, the leaders stopped indiscriminately "fighting fires" and started to empower their teammates to run the business in a more deliberate manner. The senior leaders began thinking strategically about the future. This included investing in more development programs for all levels of the team. Most importantly, the senior leaders started looking at the following year to add more clarity and structure to the team. By this time, everyone understood the importance of structure and organization.

GAMEPLAN FOR SUCCESS: THE EAGLES FULL YEAR PLAN

Like many business functions, my team struggled with too many meetings. As a result, there was not enough time to appreciate members of the team during holidays and other special times of the year. Holidays are a good excuse to make work and life fun by doing things out of the ordinary. The team performed great operationally during the high-volume peak seasons, but we continued to miss important celebrations like Mother's Day and Father's Day. As a result, I worked with the leaders to develop an SOP detailing all the dates and times that are important throughout the year. We called it the "Gameplan for Success: The Eagles Full Year Plan." The purpose of this document was to provide guidance for the year on a monthly basis. There was a breakdown of each month with details of what the month entailed and who was involved. It was important to be organized and divide the responsibilities among the team members. As a leadership team, we must be excellent in the ordinary (basics of the business).[13] Having a smooth, engaging team meeting and a well decorated hallway during holidays are small things that have an enormous impact on the morale of a team. These are common gestures in business that seem to go unnoticed until they are done poorly; then they become a big deal. The goal was to know every detail of the year, so that when unexpected challenges arose, we could remain in sync. It was critical to finish all four quarters of the year strong regardless of the challenges faced as a team.

The intent of the Game Plan for Success was to ensure the leaders were all on the same page with regard to providing the best experience possible for the leaders and team members in the building. Every month followed the same design. There was an event; a date; a point of contact person responsible for ensuring the task had a detailed, coordinated, and communicated plan; a budget; and ideas on what to do for the task. Mediocrity in planning was not acceptable. We planned for success and we executed to accomplish the mission. The SOP included the dates of weekly meetings, dates and times of the monthly All Leader Meetings, holidays, grassroots sessions, general meetings with the team members, new team member appreciation lunches, safety meetings, cookouts, Peak Seasons, and other special events. I had a great volunteer who took on the tedious task of sending the important dates for the whole year to the leaders via email so everyone had them on their calendars as a reminder. During their regular meetings, the senior leaders discussed the events occurring that month, who was responsible, and how the plan to execute would occur. This ensured the tasks were top of mind.

The Gameplan for Success added a layer of structure the leaders and teams appreciated. The positive results showed in the high level of engagement by everyone on the team. It enabled the leaders to show heartfelt appreciation to the rest of the team for all the hard work and dedication to the vision they put in. In order to aid the Gameplan for Success document and keep the team laser focused on the vision and goals, I developed a weekly guidance sheet that I sent to the leaders. The intent of the document was to provide more communication to the leaders while they juggled all the different daily tasks. Through this weekly document, I highlighted upcoming events on the Gameplan for Success, areas within the business to improve, and administrative details. Leaders printed the document and carried it with them. There is an example in the Appendix of what the weekly guidance sheet looked like. Having structure and good organization on a team provides clarity, and clarity allows those you lead to see the vision and take action to move the business forward.

KEY TAKEAWAYS OF CHAPTER 5:

In Chapter 5, I discussed the importance of structure and organization to building a team. I explained ways to bring this to life in a real world setting and how it applies. My hope is that you will take what resonated with you and apply it when building your own team.

1. Make your bed in the morning in order to build momentum for the tasks and challenges you will face throughout the day.

2. Standard Operating Procedures provide a structurally sound one consistent way of accomplishing a task.

3. Everyone on the team must operate the same way. There should be no rogue teams and individuals performing tasks not aligned to the SOPs in place.

4. There are Four Stages of Team Development. All teams go through these stages on their way to high performance.

5. Figure a way to get everyone on the same page. Many times you need to bring the team back to the basics.

6. There is a right way to roll out a program. Sending an email and expecting everyone to buy into the program is not enough.

CHAPTER SIX:

PUTTING TOGETHER THE PUZZLE

"Out of clutter, find simplicity. From discord, find harmony. In the middle of difficulty lies opportunity."

~ Albert Einstein

AFTER YOU, AS the leader (regardless of the size of the team), establish trust and credibility, it is critical to tie together everything you are trying to achieve. Solidifying a vision, setting high but achievable goals, and implementing structure involves prioritizing and executing. Jocko Willink is the best in the business when it comes to explaining this concept. I borrowed shamelessly from him to teach and implement this concept. Jocko is a retired Navy Seal Commander and expert in real world leadership. He has written two amazing books, *Extreme Ownership* and *The Dichotomy of Leadership* and has a top 100 podcast. One of the leadership concepts he explains in detail is "Prioritize and Execute." Jocko says:

> *Even the greatest of battlefield leaders could not handle an array of challenges simultaneously without being overwhelmed. That risked failing at them all. I had to remain calm, step back from my*

immediate emotional reaction, and determine the greatest priority for the team. Then, rapidly direct the team to attack that priority. Once the wheels were in motion and the full resources of the team were engaged in that highest priority effort, I could then determine the next priority, focus the team's effort there, and then move on to the next priority. I could not allow myself to be overwhelmed. I had to relax, look around, and make a call. That was what Prioritize and Execute was all about.[1]

Whether it is the military or business world, whether it is life or death or a business challenge, the concept remains the same: you cannot solve all problems and issues all at the same time by yourself. Especially in a turn-around team-building situation, there are going to be a lot of issues that seem like the top priority. However, not everything can be most important. When everything is important, nothing is important. When everything is a priority, nothing is a priority. Not all issues can be fixed or adjusted all at the same time. You need to determine what the priority is for your particular situation, then put your focus into executing and completing that priority item before moving onto something else.

As the team develops the vision and sets the goals, it is important to decide which changes that occur within the business are the highest priority, rank them, and begin to address those first. Aligning the priorities with your leaders will provide clarity as to the direction the team is taking, and ultimately set the team up for success as you begin to implement structure for the basic elements of the business. Remember, you cannot do everything all at once, which means you have to say "no" to certain ideas and fixes. If there is one thing I have learned in my career, it is that knowing when to say "no" is just as important as knowing when to say "yes".

Setting the priorities is the easy step; execution is the most difficult and crucial. Think of it this way: You build trust with your team, align to a vision, plaster your goals all over the walls, and write standard operating procedures that explain the one consistent way to accomplish a task, but it all will yield zero results if the task was not executed properly. All of that was for nothing. I told my team on a consistent basis the phrase, "You get one point for planning and nine points for execution."[2] It is so true: the planning of Operation Overlord, better known as the D-Day invasion, took over a year prior to the execution date of June 6, 1944. There were several leaders and countries involved. The weather, time of the year, and tides all played a role in the planning. Would June 6 be a day of remembrance if the Allies failed to execute the mission and overtake the beaches of Normandy? No, all that planning would have been for nothing without proper execution. Oh, and by the way, the leaders who planned the mission were NOT the ones executing the mission. Churchill, Roosevelt, and Eisenhower were never on the beaches of France. The plan had to be simple, clear, and detailed enough for every soldier from the Marines to the British to the Paratroopers, and from the Generals to the Captains to the Sergeants and Privates to understand. All had to play their parts and execute their roles.

USING ANALOGIES: NATIONAL TREASURE/ED HARRIS EXAMPLE

In the beginning, we struggled to do all the little things right, follow the Standard Operating Procedures, effectively communicate, and execute the operation. I used many analogies and stories to get my points across to my leaders. One story in particular stands out as one I told over and over again and eventually got "roasted" for by the leaders when I left (I consider getting roasted as a way of showing it worked). There is a scene in the movie National Treasure 2, where Ed Harris (the actor) was the bad guy forcing Nicholas Cage (the actor) and his friends into Mount Rushmore to find treasure. They find themselves on a big flat rock balanced precariously on top of another pointed rock. The four characters had to work together (regardless of whether or not they liked one another) to balance the rock and get out of the situation safely. Nicholas Cage and the other two characters attempt to get off the rock first, but Ed Harris's character immediately disrupts the balance and tells the other three that he must go first because he does not trust them. I showed the scene to my leaders and said:

Imagine what happens when one leader/teammate decides to not follow the basic structures within the Standard Operating Procedures. It knocks the team out of balance. If the standard says to clean the building before the end of the shift and put away all the equipment in the right spot with the batteries charged, but a leader allows the team to cut a corner that day/night because it was a long shift and his/her team needed a break, the operation gets out of balance. The next shift and team have to pick up the slack of the previous team, which puts them behind scheduled. An unclean building leads to potential safety hazards that could get someone hurt. And the cycle continues. This is the importance of keeping the operation and the team in balance. Do not be the Ed Harris that causes the team to get out of balance.

This is why you get nine points for execution. Execution is hard to do because it requires everyone on the team doing their part. Despite the fact that planning only receives one point, the plan still has to be correct and detailed enough to even have a chance at successful execution. I truly believe this is where many companies and teams fail when they try to go down the road of building a championship-caliber team. They do not put all the pieces together. The leaders want instant results, increased performance, and a better P&L immediately. Leaders can conceivably get quick results this way, but it is not sustainable. The team will end up right back where it started, which is as a low-performing team. Going through the four stages of team development takes time, energy, focus, and proper execution of your priorities. When you are the one leading this process, it is critical for you to understand from the leader above you if there are priorities you must take into consideration because those considerations might dictate the path you take. In addition, it might help you understand if you are the right leader for the job. This process is hard. Building a team is hard work; it requires a lot of patience and belief in what you are trying to accomplish. You will feel like you are alone on an island at times, but your team members need you to keep them focused on the priorities. Get a mentor who is not part of the team, who you can talk to about the challenges you face. Read books by authors who built successful teams in their careers. Listen to a podcast on leadership and team building. These are all ways that can help you increase your confidence on this journey.

JIGSAW PUZZLE: DIAGNOSING THE EAGLES

As I said in the previous chapter, the eight pages of notes I took when I joined the team were consolidated into a priority list in order to tackle the most critical areas of the business first. Regardless of your age or intellectual capacity, when you purchase a jigsaw puzzle and dump it onto the kitchen table, everyone takes a very similar approach to putting it together. First, you find the border and corner pieces and assemble the perimeter. That becomes the foundation from which the rest of the puzzle is completed. Second, you look for the most easily identifiable objects within the picture. Perhaps it is the face of a person or a dog in the picture that has easy pieces to find. In the end, what is left is the most difficult part of the puzzle: that space where the pieces are all the same color and there is nothing that distinguishes one piece from another. This is why everyone saves that section for last.

Developing a team or entering a turnaround situation is no different than putting together a jigsaw puzzle. Spend the first part of your time identifying the easiest or most critical area to improve that will have the largest impact before moving onto other areas of the business. In the case of the Eagles, the safety rating within the building was unacceptable. The hourly team members had emotional injuries and I truly believed they were trying to get the attention of the leadership team. Through their actions, the team members were saying, "Listen to us! We are not happy, and we do not know what else to do but go to the hospital for a paper cut." The team members were not bad people or bad workers; they needed to understand the expectation and be led to do the right thing. Safety made up the corners and border sections of our jigsaw puzzle.

Within the first month, I made it clear that it was not okay to work unsafely. I had a catch-phrase: "If you cannot work safely, then you cannot work here." This did not mean that I fired team members because they got hurt. I made it clear that performing unsafe acts and putting others' lives at risk would not be tolerated. My leaders had a "Safety Behavior Map" developed by one of my senior leaders that indicated what teams were unsafe and, more specifically, which team members had a history of unsafe behaviors. As a result of this tool, we implemented a high-risk program to change these unsafe behaviors.

INSTITUTIONALIZING THE FIX: HIGH-RISK PROGRAM

This high-risk program was not a scare tactic, it was a way for the senior leaders, including myself, to get involved closely with the hourly team members on the floor. It was also another avenue for me to promote the importance of safety. Every operational team preaches about safety, but when it truly comes down to it, operational metrics trump safety every time, because having a safe team is a "long game" play, especially in a "turnaround" where many leaders do not have the patience or the discipline to make it happen. The "Safety Behavior Map" identified high risk behaviors using a formula on Microsoft Excel to show safety trends based on the size of the team, the year, each team member's years of service, and the injury by type. We were able to analyze the tool, which showed there were team members who had worked for the company for two years and had been injured six times. Using the spreadsheet, we graphed out a trend of when they got hurt and predicted the next potential injury. It is important to note that there was a significantly high percentage of team members who were safety conscious and never had an injury in 20 years. Still, there were team members who were extremely unsafe and participated regularly in poor behaviors which put others at risk of being injured. In addition, there were team members who used an injury as a way to extend a vacation or get out of working, which is not productive. By using this tool, it confirmed and highlighted the areas of the team that required focus and attention.

After the senior leaders identified the high-risk team members and leaders, we developed a packet and program to follow for six months. The high-risk team member sat down in a low-threat environment with his/her direct-line leader where the leader explained in very clear detail the reason the team member was placed in the program. In addition, the leader explained to the high-risk team member the program length and expectations. At first, program members thought we were building a case for firing them, but we strove to convince them that we only wanted their unsafe habits to change. In the interest of transparency, trust, and credibility, we showed the high-risk team members the data we had as proof that they belonged in the program and outlined the steps we were implementing to help them keep their jobs and improve their standing.

Next, the high-risk team member met with his/her senior leader to emphasize the importance of the program, and allow the team member to ask questions. Lastly, I sat down with every high-risk team member to inform him/her of my commitment to the vision, to the team, and to his/her family to ensure a working environment where everyone made it home safely. I followed up with the team members every month. Out of 700 hourly team members, the high-risk program had roughly 40 team members who participated at the start. This was the first step and these were the actions the team took to commit to changing the safety culture of the DC.

BEING MORE SAFE INCREASES OPERATIONAL EFFICIENCY

Many times when teams within companies struggle to perform, they blame their failures on circumstances they believe to be out of their control. This evasion is often cultivated by the leadership team. Whenever leaders start to hear comments like,

> *"This team is just different."*
> *"This company is just different."*
> *"We are too fast paced as a team and are set up for failure."*

they need to take a deeper look into how the day-to-day activities operate. For example, when I first joined my team, there were 650 hourly team members and three different shifts (two weekday shifts and one weekend) and not enough equipment for employees to perform their job functions well. The warehouse aisles were small, but the grocery volume (in cases) was one of the largest in the network. Because my building serviced seven different states in the Southeast and Puerto Rico, the business was busy 24/7, 364 days a year. Every leader was fire-fighting each day just trying to survive. They drove the hourly team members to accomplish the workload at all costs, including sacrificing safety and performance.

I sat down with the leaders to diagnose and deep dive into how the operation could be safer and more efficient while controlling what we could control. Many people want to try to control something completely out of their control. You cannot control the weather. For instance, I could not change the high customer service demand volume the building received on a daily basis. The budget did not allow us to purchase more equipment and I could not grow the building to make the aisles bigger, so we had to think differently about our circumstances. By bringing many heads together and brainstorming ideas, the team determined that an unsafe environment was created by putting too many team members into the same aisles at the same time by having several shifts overlapping. We determined this not only impacted operational efficiency, but also severely increased the risk of safety injuries and accidents. One aisle made for two to three pieces of equipment had four to six different machines because of the environment we created.

In combination with the high-risk safety program, we changed the shift and hourly team member breakdown. We examined the volume each day, and adjusted accordingly. The operational shifts changed from three to four shifts (one morning weekday, one evening weekday, one morning weekend, and one evening weekend). In addition, we adjusted the shift times during the day to allow for a proper shift-to-shift handoff (we created a one-hour buffer between shifts where no operational activities occurred) so that team members and leaders could clean up and organize the building for the incoming team. To facilitate these changes, we expanded the team from 700 to 840 hourly team members. As a result, there were fewer team members in one aisle at a time, and there was plenty of equipment for each team to use.

USING ANALOGIES: BROKEN WINDOWS THEORY

We used the structure of the SOPs to address safety issues. We also developed an accident investigation SOP to walk a leader through the proper way to determine why an accident occurred and the corresponding actions to take to correct the behavior for the future. In addition, I developed a cleaning SOP, which helped with safety and efficiency. I read a book called *Broken Windows, Broken Business* by Michael Levine, which applied the Lean Six Sigma mentality and 5S I was implementing. 5S is a structured approach to organizing a work environment where every tool has a designated location for optimal efficiency. My leaders struggled to understand the importance of putting a broom back in its proper location (broom station) after using it and ensuring the building was cleaned properly before every shift started. According to the Broken Windows Theory, it's the behavior that follows after the broom is not put back that is the problem: "That visible signs of disorder and misbehavior in an environment encourage further disorder and misbehavior, leading to serious crimes. The principle was developed to explain the decay of neighborhoods, but it is often applied to work and educational environments."[3] I worked hard to show the team that it was about discipline and ensuring that proper safety behaviors are followed. If a little task like putting a broom back to its proper location after its use is too difficult, then imagine what other areas of the business do not follow the proper standard. Imagine the potential safety issues that might occur when no one is watching. The broom stations represented the engagement of the culture and commitment to the team vision.

LEARNING BY COMPETING: SAFETY FUN PROGRAM

We will go into more detail in the next chapter, but I quickly discovered the new team members had not been trained properly, which led to unnecessary injuries and unsafe behaviors. At my company, there was not a proper training program, so we developed a practical and professional level training course to help improve safety. Lastly, the team developed high-engagement safety programs that added fun to safety awareness. We, of course, documented the program in an SOP which we could reference throughout the program, leverage the following year, or share with other teams within the company. The SOP had a simple name, Safety Fun Program (Real creative, isn't it?). It was a seven-week program organized and executed by the Safety Team. We incorporated team-engagement ideas to identify who was fully engaged and who was not.

As part of the program, we offered prizes to various teams based on percent of participation and leaders tracked their teams' engagement. For example, we had a day for each team to wear a shirt that was green. The greater number of green shirts worn to work signified a greater commitment to safety and told us which individuals were engaged in the program. If a team had more than 75% participation, then that particular team would get points toward the end prize. Another week, the teams competed to come up with a safety slogan that would be made into a banner and placed in the building for the remainder of the year. Just by submitting a slogan, the team received more points. Another example was Super Hero Day; the leaders and team members wore a super hero shirt to get points. These were simple ideas to keep the whole team engaged for more than one week or one day. I am not always a fan of prizes for safety, but this was built more around engagement of the team members, while placing safety as the focal point. The team liked it so much, we continued the program for the next several years during different times of the year.

The above mentioned actions taken to address safety are by no means all encompassing. The key when starting to put everything together is to follow the vision and goals as set forth, follow the structure put in place, have the discipline to stay the course even when it seems difficult, and continue to build upon the trust and credibility developed earlier. A good way to lose credibility is to start putting it all together and saying one thing, but doing another. If I said, "If you cannot work safely, then you cannot work here" while our safety injuries increased, then looked the other way when poor safety behaviors were identified, I would lose all credibility, and the team would slide back into the old ways of doing things.

PERFORMANCE: EASY PICTURE IN THE PUZZLE–TACTICAL PLANNING

As soon as the safety behaviors began to improve and injuries decreased, I shifted focus to improving performance because many of the safety adjustments we made aligned to performance efficiency increases. Performance was the next step in the puzzle; the easy image with distinguishable markings.

As mentioned a few times in the book, there was a mentality of just completing the workload and getting through the day. The leaders came into the building 10 minutes prior to the shift start time and took a completely opposite approach to Lean Six Sigma. The operation started and they began making tactical decisions by reacting to the issues thrown at them. For you football fans, think of the outcome if an offensive football team broke the huddle with no play and no understanding of the plan. The chances of gaining a yard, first down, or touchdown become significantly reduced. This was how my leaders approached the day. To change this mentality, I worked with the team members to develop a tool to help them plan their days. In its most basic form, the tool was a simple Microsoft Excel sheet that allowed the leader to type in the number of cases expected for the day, and from that, the program provided them the number of hours needed to complete the day with a certain number of hourly team members. I called this simple process *Tactically Planning* the day.

As I began to put the structure in place, I realized the team was unable to execute the most basic functions of running an operation. I talked about the Back-to-Basics SOP solution in an earlier chapter. A large portion of that SOP informed the leader of how to properly plan the day. It started with coming into the building at least one hour prior to the start of the shift in order to understand how the previous shift/team was doing. It provided an opportunity to gather the information to be successful for the day, and prepare talking points to communicate to the team in order to start on time.

When I first developed the tool with my team and started to validate it, the leaders dug in their heels and of course said, "We have always just come in and finished the day, so why do we need to change?" I pointed out that on some days, leaders failed to meet their business goals, and on other days they far exceeded their goals. When I asked what the difference was, the ownership consistently fell on the hourly team members or external circumstances out of the leader's control (more on 100% ownership and how this was ingrained into the team in a later chapter). Mainly, because they did not fully understand the role or their impact (positive or negative), the leaders struggled to tell me the details of their jobs. I decided to hold an All Leader Meeting to teach the importance of tactical planning.

INCORPORATING THE TOOL: CHOOSE YOUR WEAPON

In the All Leader Meeting, I had a big bullseye on a board at one end of the room. On the other end was a table with three nerf guns: one with three darts, one handgun, and one sniper rifle. I explained the mission was to hit the middle of the bullseye. To the left was bad, to the right was bad; anywhere but the center was not good because the center represented perfection and mission accomplishment. I asked a few volunteers from the leadership team to choose only one weapon/tool for hitting the bullseye. Of course, most chose the sniper rifle. I asked why each individual chose the sniper rifle; all agreed it was the best tool out of the three to provide the best chance to hit the bullseye consistently. We had some fun with trying to hit the bullseye, and then I compared this exercise to planning the day using the tactical sheet as a tool/weapon.

The tactical sheet represented the sniper rifle that accurately depicted performance outcomes and showed potential shortcomings before they occurred. The handgun and darts represented the old way of shooting from the hip. They might get lucky in hitting the bullseye every once in a while, but more often than not, they would miss the mark. And missing the mark is missing the goal for the day. Even if they outperformed one day, there was a good chance they would underperform the next, which would result in a negative outcome for the week. Tactically planning the day enabled the leaders to be more proactive, plan for contingencies, and know ahead of time what the day might look like. In addition, it eliminated excuses and provided justification for the day.

For example, a good leader "inspects what he/she expects," so if the expectation is to hit the goals a team set out to achieve, then the leader should inspect the team to determine if they would be able to meet the expectation.

Scenario 1:

> **Patrick**: "I see you achieved your performance metric (cases in within a specified time period). How did you do that?"

> **Leader**: "We just had good volume today. The team was excited for the weekend."

> **Patrick**: "What specific actions did you take to achieve this great performance? It sounds like you just got lucky and tomorrow could yield entirely different results. I would like to know what you did so we can replicate it elsewhere on the team or company."

> **Leader**: "I do not think I did anything. We just had a good day."

Does it sound like this leader knows his/her business? Does this leader exhibit his/her worth and value? I personally do not think that it does, and this represents the old culture and old way of doing things. This represents using darts to hit a target–not very accurate.

Scenario 2:

> **Patrick:** "I see you achieved your performance metric (cases in within a specified time period). How did you do that?"

Leader: "When I came in for the day, I noticed the team prior was having a good day and would finish early, so I talked to the other team leader to ensure all the equipment was staged, fueled, and ready for my team. Then, I leveraged our tactical planning tool to insert the volume, and decided to run the operation lean, with three fewer team members. I called three team members before they left for work to see if they wanted to come into work. Two of them did not and one did, so I asked my counterparts if they needed help and they did, so I told that team member to report to another team to help out. Through the tactical planning, I noticed that if my team could perform 2% better as a team than they do on average, then I could get them out earlier to see their families, and save on efficiencies."

Patrick: "Wow, there is a lot of great information in what you just said. First, thank you for taking care of your team members and being proactive. Second, thank you for taking care of the business. You came into the building early and ensured a proper handoff. Is this something that would be beneficial for the rest of the team?"

Leader: "Yes, I think I can make the operation safer and more efficient."

Patrick: "Would you mind taking ownership over putting together a plan that you could present to the other teams to potentially put this into an SOP and develop one consistent way of operating?"

Leader: "Yes, of course."

Does it sound like this leader knows his/her business? Does this leader exhibit his/her worth and value? Does this leader understand the vision and goals? Does this leader have ownership in the success or failure of the team? These were true conversations I had with my team, which led to additional shifts and a structured parking plan/shift-to-shift handoff plan. This all came about because the leaders began to look at their days, weeks, months, quarters, and years through a tactical lens. The leaders began to see the big picture. The first scenario represents a true conversation I had with a manager who did not last long with the team. It was not because he was a bad person. He just wanted to come into the building the same way as the last 20 years without moving the business forward or taking care of his team properly.

Team members do not come to work wanting to do a bad job. They want to do the best job they can. It is the leaders' job to give their team members tools to be successful, and planning is one of those tools. I do not think there are many aspects in life where planning is a bad thing. Smart people plan financially for their future. They plan their careers in detail. They think about how they want to raise their children. Why would you not want to plan out your day and set the expectations for your team?

Giving my leaders the tools to be successful was critical. This gave ownership of the business to the leaders and allowed them to think about how to make the operation more efficient. The development of a tactical planning SOP generated many ideas, and more importantly, boosted the performance more than 10%. This helped teammates buy into the vision and goals, and generated momentum. This was not a profound idea I brought to the team. It was part of putting it all together, listening to what the team members were saying, and taking action. I like to think that my job was to prioritize and execute the important elements of the business.

MORE IMPACTFUL IMAGES IN THE PUZZLE: DEVELOPMENT PROGRAM
The next step in completing the puzzle–after the safety behaviors and performance efficiency improved–was creating impactful development programs which would ultimately improve morale. Diving into the details of the business and addressing the safety concerns improved operational efficiency, but one of the biggest insights gained from addressing safety first

was that our team members had not been properly trained from day one of walking into the building. This, we found, was a serious problem; if, on the day a team member joins the team, she/he has a trainer who exhibits the following behaviors, we are in big trouble and behind the power curve of trust:

- Hates his/her job

- Distrusts the leadership team

- Trains off of "experience" versus a proven method of work (one consistent way)

- Negative attitude

- Unsafe behaviors

- Individual mindset vs a team mentality

- Feels slighted by the leadership team

This type of team member is toxic and one of the biggest barriers that you, as the leader, will come across. They are the face of the team. It does not matter what you do; if this is the type of person training your new-hire team members, progress will be difficult...if not impossible.

We implemented many programs within my leadership team, which included Path to Leadership, Area Leader High Potential, and Safety Team Member Programs, but the program that had the largest impact on the future of the team was the Eagle Elite Program. During this time period in the journey (Norming Phase), I pushed for 100% ownership of the business at every level within the team. When it came down to it, I had to put actions to my words. Our hourly team member trainers had to be trained properly and be an extension of the leadership team; meaning, they must be empowered to influence business decisions.

Every person is different in his/her learning. Some learn things fast while others learn more slowly. The old training programs the HR department developed were time-based. They assumed that if a team member was trained for three weeks, he/she should know everything about the business and should know how to perform his/her job. The problem with time-based training is that it forces the trainers to sign off on an individual who might not be ready, which causes anxiety and frustration, potentially leading to safety injuries or performance issues, and ultimately to that team member leaving the team and company. This leads to high turnover and more team members sharing the brunt of the workload, which leads to potentially more injuries and poorer performance. It is a vicious cycle. We decided to train the new hires the right way from day one, celebrate their progress, and sign off on the training after they were fully trained, not before.

I was fortunate to have a highly engaged senior leader on my team who took the idea of an Eagle Elite and made it a reality. It was a professional level course; three full days of training on leadership, teaching, the business, the vision, the goals, the Playbook, safety, quality, performance, and development. It was taught by many of the senior leaders in the building. Safety procedures were taught by the senior safety leader on the team. I taught leadership and the vision. Quality procedures and their importance was taught by the senior quality leader. The performance of the job function was taught by leaders who had performed that same job for years prior to getting into leadership and knew that the best practices only derived from experience and performing the job the way the company intended. There was a test at the end. Individuals who did not pass did not become an Eagle Elite.

Instead of having 100 "T3 Trainers (old trainers' system)," we had 50 highly engaged, proud trainers called "Eagle Elites." They were extensions of the leadership team. Many were team members who were part of the other development programs and had influence on the floor with the hourly team members. This program decreased our turnover rate from 55% to less than 25%. As with everything the team did, there was an SOP developed, which enabled us to share our program with other teams within the company. This provided another pipeline from which to pull leaders and develop them. This program ended up feeding the Path to Leadership program and provided opportunities for mid-level leaders to gain experience in teaching a class and making an impact on the team so they could reach other levels within the organization.

Prior to leaving the team, I remember talking to a new hire who had been on the team for fewer than three weeks. She told me, "My Eagle Elite has been great. I understand the vision of the team and the importance of my role, and I believe everyone on the team has my best interest at heart." The Eagle Elites team members had great attitudes which segued into a positive impact on the new hires. This was a big deal because there were so many supply chain competitors in the area competing for good operations specialists. There were 10 different distribution centers within 50 miles of our team. We paid well, but we put our stock in developing our teammates properly.

THE DARK COLOR IN THE CORNER OF THE PUZZLE: QUALITY

In every puzzle, there is a portion that is all the same color and poses a lot of difficulty. This is the area of the business that usually takes more time to improve. For the Eagles, this puzzle portion was "quality." In an operational environment, quality involves not damaging the products, inventory management, ensuring the products flow through the building properly, load securement, and product stacking and wrapping. It requires discipline by everyone involved. We saved this element of the turnaround for last because structure and discipline had to be in place before we could fix the quality within the building.

Taking a data-driven approach was the best way to track improvements. There are three main functions within a distribution center that make up the majority of the operation and each can have its own impact on quality: inbound operations, order filling/replenishments, and outbound operations.

For inbound operations, a vendor–let's say a meat company–backs a truckload of chicken in the door. The team members unload the truck, count the cases to ensure we receive what we agreed to pay for, haul the pallets to an aisle in the building, and put the pallets away for the shipping team to eventually ship to the store. Any shortcuts taken during inbound by the team will negatively affect the quality for a very long time, which then causes a lot of wasted time and labor hours. There are any number of errors that could occur. For example, a team member could miscount the pallets and cases, scan the wrong pallet and put the wrong label on a pallet, or put the pallet away in the wrong location. There is a proper and correct way to perform every job function within the team, but complacency and poor discipline can derail even the best system.

For order filling/replenishment operations, the team members drive on electrical power jacks placing cases on pallets while attempting to achieve the perfect stack like they are playing Tetris. There is a warehouse system that tells them which aisles to drive down, which cases to place on their pallet, and which door to drop the pallet at to be loaded onto a trailer. When a slot on the ground is empty, a replenishment driver on a fork-lift pulls a full pallet from the racks in the air to place on the ground. This part of the operation is where the majority of the team works. Many quality issues can occur here. Orderfillers can pick the wrong number of cases and/or damage the products. If the warehouse system tells the team member to pick up three cases and he/she only picks two, the system does not record the difference, so the inventory in the building is wrong.

During loading operations, team members wrap the pallets of stacked cases in shrink wrap using a big machine, and load the pallets onto a trailer to be taken to the stores. This process creates more opportunities for cases to be damaged or loaded poorly, potentially causing safety or quality issues at the store. Every team member has the potential to impact the quality of the next person's work within the operation.

To get my point across to the team, I charted the journey of a single case and showed how many team members touch it before it gets to the customer. There are a lot of touch points, which is why quality is so important, but also difficult to control. This is why taking a data-based approach was the best way to identify which teams struggled and who followed procedure and who did not. The leaders examined different metrics for each of the three portions of the operation. We placed the main focus on the data from the inbound end of the operations because if it is wrong from this point, it will trickle through to the end. Once we identified the shortcuts being used by team members and which shifts/teams they came from, we addressed it by explaining the whole impact these errors had on the business. We explained the "why" to them. We put some programs and procedures in place, and then tracked the data. Once we had a solid procedure, this SOP became part of the Playbook.

We took this same approach into the rest of the operation. If your team is not in an operational role similar to this, our process may still be helpful to you. Try to look at the big picture of your business from a quality perspective. There are quality checks in marketing, finance, operations, sales, and procurement. Use data to point the team in the right direction, but most importantly, look at the whole team from the perspective of putting it all together. I did not rush into making changes when I first joined the team. Many leadership books promote this concept because when examining a business, it becomes tempting to make immediate changes because some of the problems/issues seem so obvious. Instead, identify the areas that need to be changed to make the biggest impact. Prioritize the areas critical to improvement, then execute the plan.

KEY TAKEAWAYS OF CHAPTER 6:

In Chapter 6, I demonstrated how to break down the areas of the team that need the most focus by comparing it to a jigsaw puzzle. Remember, every team is different and not every team has the same challenges. Leverage the concepts in the chapter to help guide you in your business.

1. One point for planning, nine points for execution. Execution is hard because it requires discipline to follow the plan through to the end to achieve results.

2. Prioritize and execute the things that make sense to build your team and move the business forward.

3. Watch for the excuses made for circumstances the team finds themselves in. Do not be afraid to address them and call them what they are.

4. Control what you can control.

5. Building a team is like putting together a jigsaw puzzle. Put together the border or frame for the eventual structure, then work inward, assembling the most obvious pieces first.

CHAPTER SEVEN:

DEVELOPMENT PROGRAMS

"A lot of people have gone further than they thought they could because someone else thought they could."

~ Zig Zigler

ONE OF MY FAVORITE quotes as it relates to the development of individuals comes from Henry Ford. Ford says, "The only thing worse than training your employees and having them leave is not training them and having them stay."[1] If you invest in your team, your team will be better off in the long run. In order to create a pipeline of leaders ready to take the reins, I recognized that every individual teammate was at a different level in his/her career journey. Some teammates had no desire to be a leader on the team, which is fine. There are no issues with great teammates who will do what is asked of them and give 100% effort. There are individuals who have a strong desire to be a leader, but are early in the journey and need a mentor to help guide them. Some individuals are much further along, and require advanced training to be the best leader possible. Lastly, there are leaders influencing others, who need mentorship and training to get to another level of leadership. I taught leadership development using the Toyota

Four Stages of Leader Development:[2]

1. No desire to be a leader

2. Desire to be a leader, but too early in their career

3. Desire to be a leader, and has actual leadership experience, but needs to tie it all together

4. Is a leader, influencing a team in a positive way who needs mentorship to grow

I followed these four stages of leadership development when teaching the Eagles team. Through my interactions with hourly team members, mid-level leaders, and senior leaders, I recognized pretty quickly where each member fell within the journey. The issue I found was that the individuals themselves did not recognize where they were in the journey. Some hourly team members believed they were ready for a leadership role but did not exhibit the maturity or skills required to have the awesome responsibility of leading others. I had direct conversations with these individuals. These were tough conversations, but necessary for those individuals to grow. The same was true for many of my leaders. Many leaders believed they "deserved" a promotion because they had worked for a long time at the same level or had several years of service with the company. I explained that taking on more responsibility is about influence and the impact a leader makes on those they serve. Leadership is earned, not given because of length of service. Companies that adopt a policy of promoting because of length of service will fail in the long run.

Through my conversations and teaching, I discussed the following elements from the four stages of leadership development:[3]

1. **Self-Development**: Natural leaders see possibilities for improvements in self and others. This compares ability with potential. An individual in this phase relies on mentors to help guide them. They read books on leadership

development (self-help), and take leadership courses. In Pat Williams' book, *Leadership Excellence*, there are seven sides of learnable leadership:[4]

a. Vision

b. Communication Skills

c. People Skills

d. Character

e. Competence

f. Boldness

g. Servanthood

These are all areas an individual can focus their attention to develop oneself.

2. **Coach & Develop Others** (Helping others self-develop): This phase is when an individual learns to see strengths and weaknesses in others. They develop next-generation leaders. Teaching and developing others are keys to a leader's growth. A perfect example is seen through the mentorship tree of Socrates. Socrates mentored Plato who mentored Aristotle who mentored Alexander the Great.[5] Colin Powell said, "Leadership is motivating people, turning people on, getting 110% out of a personal relationship." A leader must be willing to invest in others.

3. **Support Daily Kaizen**: Kaizen means continuous improvement. Leaders continuously identify gaps that prevent themselves and/or the team from achieving goals and targets.

4. **Create Vision & Align Goals**: Initiate and sustain con-

tinuous improvement through visual management of goals. This fourth phase is—when leaders focus on problem-solving and developing people. This is when a leader is like a captain of a ship; creating a vision and ensuring the team is set up for success when the leader is no longer directing the team.

In order to grow the team, I developed four leadership programs with my leaders. Some of the programs existed in the company prior to me; however, they were ineffective at providing opportunities for growth. This is a quick overview of each program as it is related to the leadership journey:

1. **Develop-to-Lead Program**–We developed this program for the Self-Development and Coach and Develop Others phases. We based the design upon an established program within the company. This program was just as much for the mid-level leadership team as it was for the curious hourly team members looking to be a leader on the team. Each of the 60 leaders got paired with an hourly team member (who expressed interest in leadership) to mentor. The leader created lesson plans with his/her mentee. There was an SOP document that provided ideas such as reading books together, discussing podcasts, creating SMART goals, building resumes, perfecting interview skills, or discussing leadership topics. The leaders met with their mentees for an hour during working time at least once per month. This provided insight into how serious the team member was about developing and advancing his/her career. This Develop-to-Lead program fed the more advanced Path to Leadership Program.

2. **Path to Leadership Program**–The design of this program was to create leaders of character. Candidates had to participate in a rigorous process to get selected. Out of 900 hourly team members, only five got selected per class. The class was six months in length with

varying tasks to accomplish in order to graduate. Each potential candidate submitted a packet to the senior leadership team, which consisted of a written essay on leadership, resume, and a completed questionnaire. I reviewed every packet to provide feedback on all three. Each team member who submitted a packet conducted an interview in front of a panel of senior leaders. The panel consisted of myself and two other senior leaders within the team. The questions in the interview were designed to find candidates who were humble, hungry, and smart based on Patrick Lencioni's book, *The Ideal Team Player*, which provided suggestions on how to choose talent.[6] After all the interviews, the panel collected feedback, ranked the candidates, and selected only five to be in the class. Regardless of whether we selected a candidate or not, he/she received valuable, straightforward feedback on his/her resume and interview in order to improve for the future. Each Path to Leadership team member paired with an Operations Manager (Senior Leader) to be his/her mentor. The classes centered around leadership, the business, and character building. The team members delivered presentations in front of peers, worked on projects within the building that could potentially impact the business, spent a day at a store with the customers in order to understand a different side of the business, and received live feedback on proper ways to interview. Many team members earned the honor of leading others through a promotion to the salaried leadership team. This became the pipeline from which many new leaders were chosen.

3. **Area Leader High Potential Program**: This program followed a similar structure to the Path to Leadership program. The packets, submissions, interviews, and selection process were the same but candidates were held to a much higher standard. Out of 45 mid-level leaders, we only selected three. The program lasted six months and focused on leadership and project development—as well as thinking differently about problems and the business. We sent each

member to a two-week Lean Six Sigma Green Belt course at a local University.

4. **Eagle Elite Training Program**: I discussed the details of this program in the puzzle analogy in Chapter 6, so I will not dive further into this impactful program. This program was the last developed and we created it to teach the trainers how to be trainers. This was all about empowering our trainers to make decisions with the best interest of the team in mind. The trainers became an extension of the leadership team. One of my most trusted senior leaders developed and taught the whole program, which was ultimately rolled out to several distribution centers within the company. This was a one-week course that taught leadership, safety, quality, the business, the operation, teaching techniques, evaluations, and proper procedures for each job function within the team.

OWNERSHIP: DEVELOP OTHERS TO TAKE OVER

When you take over for a new team, if you are the smartest person on the team, you have a problem. All great leaders who have led successful teams were influenced by people who thought differently than they did, and had smarter individuals advising them to make decisions. These great leaders constantly thought about who would replace them when they moved on. The past chapters centered around building the team and ensuring the proper trajectory for success. This chapter is about the importance of your legacy and the programs you put in place to ensure future success without you.

The mark of a good leader is not how well the team does when he/she is there to lead it, it is how well the team does after she/he is gone. Does the team immediately go back to the old ways of running the business? Does all the discipline you thought you instilled fall apart? Does performance and team engagement decrease? Some managers will say, "You see, I left the team and they failed. I was the glue that held them together. I was the reason they were successful." I can promise you; this is not the right mindset of a person having the awesome responsibility of leading a team. If your team fails when you are not there, then all you have is a bunch of "yes men/women" who only did what you said because of your rank and title. They did not truly believe in the vision, the goals set forth, or the structure you put in place. You built zero trust and credibility with the team. If you were to revisit a team 5-10 years after you left and the team still had the same swagger about moving the business, then you can say you helped make an impact.

In order for you to leave a legacy and ensure your team "takes off like a rocket ship," build development programs at all levels within the team. This seems like a simple process, yet companies fail over and over in this phase of team-building. Companies send one or two people to get MBAs or conduct e-Learnings online where the only accountability is whether the person clicked through all the slides. Rarely do you see the highest levels of the leadership team truly engaged. Sure, the leaders will endorse the program, yet they do not know who is in the program or invest any of their time in mentoring these upcoming leaders. I am not saying the CEO or top senior leader must be the owner of the development program, but I am saying he/she must have serious involvement in it for it to be successful.

BACK ON "THE BUS": HIRE THE RIGHT PEOPLE

Development starts with the talent you bring onto the team, what kind of culture you are building, and ultimately the hiring process. If you are hiring for only the roles you have open, then you will not get the talent you are seeking. You should always hire a person into the company who is capable of growing into two roles above the one for which he/she was initially hired. As I mentioned earlier, Patrick Lencioni has a great book called *The Ideal Team Player*, which lays it out succinctly: You should hire someone who is humble, hungry, and smart.[7] This is not just at a leader level; this is everyone on your team.

Lencioni says, "The kind of people that all teams need are people who are humble, hungry, and smart: humble, being with little ego, focusing more on their teammates than on themselves. Hungry, meaning they have a strong work ethic, are determined to get things done, and contribute any way they can. Smart, meaning not intellectually smart but inner-personally smart."[8]

I touched upon some of the development programs built for the Eagles; now I would like to dive into the details of these programs to provide you with an example of how this might come to life in your organization. Before I do, it's important to look at development programs that have little impact and do not set a team up for success.

When I entered West Point, there were a few things that became immediately clear. West Point attracts some of the best and brightest minds in the country. There are a lot of valedictorians, three-sport athletes, sports team captains, club leaders, and class leaders. These kids have not endured much failure in life. On Day One (R-Day), the new cadets are stripped of these leadership identities and instead, must learn to work together as a team. New cadets are taught to put the team above themselves. They learn to be followers. Before you can lead, you must walk in the shoes of a follower/subordinate. During the first year, new cadets learn there is no one for them to lead. They have many responsibilities, but none of them involve leading. It is all about learning. They learn from upperclassmen, officers, enlisted soldiers, and instructors. In the academic classroom, the class size is small. Rarely are there more than 15 cadets in a room for a course. Preparation for class is conducted the day prior and the time spent with the instructor is used to facilitate understanding and engagement. As the cadets grow in maturity, their responsibilities grow as well. In the second year, cadets lead one or two other cadets. In the third year, they will lead anywhere from seven to forty cadets. And in the fourth year, they will lead anywhere from 40 to 4,000 (The Corps). This process is known as Crawl, Walk, Run, which is a legitimate technique that takes time, but works.

By the time I was ready to graduate and become an officer, I learned the advanced fundamentals of leadership. Now, it was time to put my leadership to the test in order to grow. This was all done in a vacuum at West Point. You could test ideas, fail, make mistakes, learn, adjust, and that was all expected. In the real world and the real Army; however, mistakes and failures happen, but sometimes there are consequences to them that there was no way to prepare for. The West Point process worked best in the small class sizes set for a learning environment and the maturation process of taking on more leadership responsibilities over time based upon how far along you were in your journey.

When I joined the company, one of the first questions I asked my boss was, "What kind of leadership programs do we have and how can I get involved?" She was ecstatic and said, "We have a great program called Develop to Lead. We have a lot of great talent in the group." Perhaps my expectations were too high, but when I went to a class, I was disappointed. The candidates were hourly workers on the team who expressed interest in becoming managers. There were 10 team members in the conference room who gave presentations to the group. There were two managers in the room, one of whom was me. I remember looking over at one of the participants and his head was on the table with eyes closed. It was straight out of a movie. I wish I was making this up. The presentations, at no fault of the individuals, were bad. There had clearly been no preparation or guidance provided. After the class, I asked the other manager, "Were you missing any candidates and are you the only manager leading the class?" She said, "We have about 50 in the class, but no one ever shows up. And we started with three other managers, but they stopped showing up."

The senior leader in the building raved about how good a program they had. Now, either she did not understand good leadership, or she was not involved at all. I know she is an amazing leader, so it must have been that she did not place a priority on the program. Out of 650 hourly team members, you should not have 50 in a class, nor should lack of attendance be acceptable.

This bothered me, so I reached out to the head of HR in our region since she was the person I talked to during my recruitment process. I asked if she could send me the program all other distribution centers in the region followed. She raved about the great programs the company offered. She called the programs "Path to Leadership," but explained she could not send me anything because there was nothing too formal. I asked if she could give me the name of a leader in another building/team who seemed to be successful at developing leaders so I could talk to him/her about the program.

I reached out to the recommended manager and she sent me information similar to what my team had utilized. Here is what the leadership development program looked like for the company:

- Answer five questions on a questionnaire

- Submit a resume with the questionnaire

- Must not have the highest accountability level on their current record

- All team members who applied were selected–typically around 40-60

- Only one or two managers lead the program

- The course was 12 months long, meeting once per month for two hours

- After 12 months, the participants got a certificate

I set a meeting with the Director of the building to ask more questions regarding leadership development programs. I asked her what the intent was behind the programs. Was it to check a box? Was it to create leaders within the building? Was it to build character? I did not receive the answers I expected, so I explained to her my thoughts and my observations. I told her what I thought a good program might look like.

I did not have much business experience because I had spent the last 12 years in a military setting. It concerned me that such a large company did not have a pipeline of team members ready to grow as leaders and influence the future teams. The only criterion I observed was entitlement for years of service. Managers and hourly team members walked around telling others they knew what was best because they accumulated 10, 15,

20, or 25 years with the company. Do not get me wrong: that has value, but those years sometimes gave the employee a reason to stop learning, stop looking at problems from different points of view, and stop challenging traditional thinking.

When I looked at the last five hourly team members within my building who got promoted to manager level or who were selected to be in the different development programs, I noticed the company did not base the selection criteria on how good a leader or influencer they were. I asked, "Why did the leadership team choose this person during the interview?" The responses were consistent:

"They had the best performance as an orderfiller."

"They did not have the best attitude, but they 'pulled' high" ('Pull' is a reference to order filling performance).

"They were the most vocal during start-up meetings." This was sometimes positive and sometimes negative.

"They have been with the company for 10 years. It was time."

I called some other teams within the region again and I noticed the same thing. Promotions were based upon years of service and performance. This intrigued me, so I dove even deeper and looked into the safety records of each of the individuals and what others had to say about them. Many—not all—had been hurt several times for poor working practices and poor discipline; meaning, they did not follow the work instructions for how the job was intended to be performed. They took shortcuts to achieve a higher performance, which in turn gave them more money through the incentive programs the company had in place. They undercut their peers in order to accomplish the high numbers, and lastly, the individuals were normally the trainers who engaged with the new team members coming into the building.

It was clear, there were no true leadership development programs. I am speaking about the programs within the company I worked for, but as I got further into my career, most of the companies I engaged with had similarly ineffective programs. They wanted to do better, but the business got in the way. Developing people is an investment. It is a very expensive investment. I used to tell people there is only one company in the world that can afford to invest $500,000 in training one person in straight leadership development for several years and that is the United States government. The military academies provide this leadership development groundwork. They are not perfect by any means, but can you imagine Google, Apple, Amazon, or Facebook sending one of their employees to school for four years to learn nothing but leadership? Yes, they send employees to get MBAs, master's degrees, and other certifications, but that is for business purposes, not straight leadership.

I believed it was my job to take the lessons I learned at West Point and the Army to put together a simple development strategy for all levels of leadership. I developed the foundation in the first building/team I led, adjusted it in the second building/team, and then significantly improved it and advanced it in my last building/team. This program can be adjusted to fit any size team in any organization. Yes, it is based upon an operational team, but a marketing team, procurement team, or consulting team could take a similar approach.

In depth: The Eagles' development program

When I joined the Eagles Team, I saw the same development program I saw in the other teams within the company. It was not effective. On any team, there are great performers and poor performers, good managers and bad managers, employees with good attitudes and bad attitudes, team members with strong educational backgrounds and some with little formal training, and some who want to be in a leadership role and some who do not. Every individual is at a different phase in his/her leadership journey, which means you need to meet all team members where they are.

As with everything involved in building this team, I started by laying out the program on paper in an SOP format. I received input from many individuals within the team and from outside the team. I had the team start to communicate the program to the hourly team members. The first program was called Path to Leadership and it was intended for hourly team members who wanted to join the leadership team and were much further in their leadership journey. There were simple requirements that had to be met in order to apply to the program. The team member could not have:

- Any severe accountability within the previous years

- A history of poor attendance at work

- Any major safety accident that indicated a record of poor safety behaviors

The team members submitted packets to their senior leaders (Operations Managers) with the following items:

- One-page essay on what it means to be a leader

- Answers to five questions about leadership

- Resume

I took all the submitted packets and reviewed them myself. Each team member who submitted a packet was interviewed. The interest in the program grew over the years, but there were normally about 20 candidates out of 800. I provided feedback on every resume with lessons I learned from a recruiting firm about resume building.

I coordinated a week to conduct the interviews and held five to seven interviews per day with two or three other senior leaders in the building. They were panel-style interviews. The panel asked four or five questions and the interviews lasted ~45 minutes. We measured everything from content, attire, and professionalism to the handshake and eye contact. Some might argue that none of this matters, but when you are trying to find the right candidates for a leadership development program, the program must be detailed and challenging.

After conducting the interviews, the panelist selected only five candidates. There were many times when six or seven candidates qualified, but we made it a point to only take five, to keep it elite. We brought in every candidate who interviewed to provide direct feedback on his/her resume, one-page paper, and interview. This whole process was time-consuming but worth every minute. The team members not selected were placed into a Develop to Lead program, which I will discuss next.

There are other selection criteria you can use in your own development program. The ones I listed made sense for my team, but adding other criteria like a letter of recommendation only strengthens your decision on which team members are ready for the next step in their journey. Below is an excerpt from the SOP that explains the program structure. Each candidate paired with an Operations Manager who mentored him/her and was present at all classes. The program lasted five months and was fast paced.

Path to Leadership Program: After the panel selects the Path to Leadership candidate, they will be notified of the date of the first class. Each class is approximately two to three hours in length. Each candidate will receive a black leadership notebook to take notes, 21 Irrefutable Laws of Leadership, a pen, and a copy of the curriculum. Below is the curriculum by month:

1. *Month 1: Meet & Greet*

    a. Each mentor and mentee will stand up to give a quick description of his/her background.

    b. The chosen champion (senior leader in the building) for the Path to Leadership Program will give a presentation on how the Path to Leadership Program will work (in detail).

    c. Exercise: Each mentee will draw out of a hat a topic to talk about. They will have a total of five minutes to prepare and then they will give a five-minute presentation to the class on that topic. The point of this exercise is to determine each mentee's level of communication skill and outside-the-box thinking. It will make the mentee uncomfortable.

d. The champion will discuss the lesson plan for the month.

2. *Month 2: 21 Irrefutable Laws of Leadership Study*

a. Each of the mentees will receive a copy of the book by John Maxwell. The chapters will be separated by the different laws for the candidates.

b. Each mentee will give a 5-10 minute presentation on his/her chapter.

c. One Operations Manager mentor will give a presentation on their leadership philosophy (5-10 minutes).

d. One mentee will be selected among all the members in the class to give the same presentation to all the leaders in the next All Leaders Meeting.

3. *Month 3: Work in a store*

a. The class will meet at a local store to conduct a tour of the back room. They will pair with the store manager. They will be at the store most of the day. The store manager will assign them to different areas of the store. They will conduct audits, unload trailers, walk with the manager, and work alongside the employees at the store. This will give the team members an idea of how our customers receive the freight from the distribution center (The Eagles).

b. When the store visit is complete class members will have two weeks to put together a presentation. They will practice in front of an Operations Manager group and then present their findings at the next General Meeting in front of the whole building.

4. ***Month 4: Interview Preparation***

a. Prior to the month 4 class, the mentor and mentee will meet to discuss the interview process. The mentor will teach the mentee about the STAR method and conduct mock interviews.

b. When the candidates come in for the class there will be a panel of three judges. The panel will ask three questions of each team member in front of everyone. At the end of each mock interview, the other mentees and mentors will critique the mentee who was interviewed. All mentees will go through the same process.

c. Each mentee will be instructed to choose a building project to work on in any department of his/her choosing. They will have just shy of two months to prepare and put together the presentation. This should be a project that will help improve elements in the building.

5. ***Month 5: Final Project Presentation***

a. Each mentee will have 20 minutes to present his/her project and findings to all the leaders in an All Leader Meeting. There will be a five-minute question and answer segment.

b. This is the culmination of the Path to Leadership Program.

Path to Leadership Results: After mentees in the Path to Leadership program graduate the five-month course, they will have the tools necessary to apply for the Area Leader role within the building. As positions open in the DC, these will be the first team members the leadership team evaluates to promote to Area Leader. Once the five-month program is complete, a new set of Operations Managers and candidates will be selected utilizing the same process.

Path to Leadership Expectations: The five candidates selected will be held to a higher standard than their peers. They will be expected to act in a professional manner at all times (on the clock and off the clock), they will be expected to dress professionally, be on time to meetings, not miss any meetings, and come prepared to class. In the event that one of these expectations is not met, it could result in removal from the program without graduating.

A program like this only works when there is leadership buy-in and engagement at all levels. There were two classes conducted a year, and at least seven of the Path to Leadership graduates moved into mid-level leadership within our team, onto other teams within the company, or to teams at other companies. Our goal was never to make leaders specific to our company, it was to develop individuals with a passion for taking care of others in order to make them better leaders; not better leaders only for our company, just better leaders. If that meant moving on to another team or company, that was okay. The engagement improved because the team members talked to each other and truly promoted the program. The hourly team members believed there was an accessible avenue for growth within the company and believed the company was taking care of them.

NURTURING THE TEAM: DEVELOP TO LEAD PROGRAM

During the creation of the Path to Leadership program, it became clear that a slower-paced program needed to be established. We created the Develop to Lead program to feed the pipeline into the Path to Leadership.

This program was just as necessary for the development of the mentors as it was for the mentees. This is an excerpt from the SOP:

Develop to Lead Overview: Every leader (Operations Manager and Area Manager) will be responsible for the development of at least one hourly team member who does not report directly to them. Each leader is required to meet with the team member once a month or more. The leader can discuss different development and work-related topics. This program is designed to allow latitude in the training and teaching of the hourly team member. It is just as much for the leader as it is for the team member. Part of being a leader is being a good teacher. This creates a comfortable environment for the leader to learn to teach and develop others.

Develop to Lead Selection Process: It is important to understand that not all team members who perform well make good leaders. Below are the selection standards associated with the Develop to Lead Program:

1. The team member must express interest in the program.

2. The team member must submit a resume to their Operations Manager. This will provide a baseline for their commitment and determine what development is required for them.

3. The team member cannot be on any accountability levels.

4. The Operations Managers will submit the names and packets at their monthly Operations Managers meeting. There is no limit to the number of candidates.

5. The Operations Managers will work with the General Manager and Human Resource Manager to rank talent levels among the candidates. Next, they will assign one candidate to an Operation Manager and Area Leader.

6. Both the candidate and leader will be notified of their start date and told the name of their mentor/mentee.

Develop to Lead Execution: The candidates who were not selected to be a part of the Path to Leadership program will have the first opportunity to be assigned a mentor in the Develop to Lead program. These team members were vetted through a more in-depth process, which makes them ideal candidates. The mentor and mentee are required to meet once a month to discuss any topic they choose. They can meet as many times as they choose; however, they will document at least one meeting per month.

Discussion Topics: Below is a list of discussion topics the mentor can explore with the mentee:

1. Establish Goals: Personal, Financial, Career

   - SMART (Specific, Measurable, Attainable, Realistic, Timeline)

2. Create an Individual Development Plan

   - Talk about your Leadership "Brand." When people think of you as a leader, what do they think about?

3. Establish a professional resume

   - Formatting, specific examples, and flow

4. Teach interview techniques

   - Conduct mock interviews
   - STAR Method (situation, task, action, result)

5. "Read a book together. This is list is found in the building leadership library (not all encompassing)

   - How to Win Friends and Influence People
   - The Leadership Challenge
   - The Servant
   - 360 Degree Leader
   - The 21 Irrefutable Laws of Leadership
   - The 5 Dysfunctions of Team
   - The Magic of Thinking Big
   - Lincoln on Leadership
   - The Oz Principle
   - The Carrot Principle

6. Set up a store opening visit

- This introduces the team member to a new level of the business and shows how we, as a DC, can affect the quality of a store.

7. Presentation Skills

- Have your mentee give you and your peers a five-minute presentation on leadership

Results: The Eagles will continue to develop talent at the hourly team member level in order to create a teaching environment and a pool of potential future leaders. Not all Develop to Lead team members will become Area Leaders; however, when the leadership team develops team members, they will use what they learn to lead their peers. In addition, they will become professional team members with the ability to better themselves and others around them.

Just as the Path to Leadership program required senior leaders' involvement and engagement, the Develop to Lead Program required the same level of commitment. Over time, this program fed the Path to Leadership program and the Path to Leadership program fed the selection of future mid-level leaders. In addition, it emphasized the vision and the Playbook. It explained to more and more leaders the "why" behind the improvements in culture and performance. However, these two programs alone were not sufficient. There is still a large leap required for leaders to continue personal growth. As a result, I developed one more leadership development program for the Area Leaders who desired to grow into Operations Managers and continue their professional journey.

MOVING UP: AREA LEADER HIGH POTENTIAL PROGRAM

I leveraged the same selection process as the Path to Leadership program and called it the Area Leader High Potential program. There were three out of 60 Area Leaders selected and the program was led and taught by me. The concept of the program was to provide relevant development opportunities, expose the leaders to different areas of the business, broaden their career paths, and enhance key leadership skills necessary to lead team members in an ever-changing work environment. The Area Leaders worked on projects that had a business impact and all earned a Lean Six Sigma Green Belt through the local university (paid for by the company). The intent of the program was for Area Leaders to think two levels above their current roles, dive into the details of the business, drive results through the use of Lean Six Sigma thinking, and enhance their communication skills. The leaders conducted most of the six-month program outside the classroom working with other leaders in the building and an assigned Senior Manager. The Area Leaders graduated with several strong bullet points to use for their professional resumes, and several specific examples of business results to utilize during the interview process.

All in all, never second guess your decision to invest in the development of your people. It will pay you back 10-fold. If you are a small company that cannot invest a lot of money, there are plenty of free online programs, books, and podcasts you can leverage. You can invest your own time to teach and develop. You can hold presentations on leadership development. I can promise you that if you just show up and make development available, at least one team member will benefit from it. Watching a team member get promoted, grow, or improve is the best feeling in the world. To know that you had a hand in making his/her life better is what being a leader is all about.

Again, the development programs described in this chapter are from the lens of an operational team, but if you think about your own team, you can utilize some of the details to create your own program. LinkedIn has many great ideas for project management, marketing, and HR professionals. Providing structure and development programs gives a level of accountability to you, as well as your team members.

KEY TAKEAWAYS OF CHAPTER 7:

In Chapter 7, I covered the importance of development programs for building a team. I explained in detail the programs we created and the results achieved. My goal is for you to take what resonated with you to create your own development programs.

1. Invest in your people. You will not regret it. As long as they are better people for being on your team, that is success.

2. Make available ways to develop individuals at different levels of their leadership journey.

3. Never think you are the smartest person on the team.

4. The mark of a good leader is how well the team does after the leader moves on.

CHAPTER EIGHT:

CHALLENGE THE STATUS QUO

"Leaders must challenge the process precisely because any system will unconsciously conspire to maintain the status quo and prevent change."

> ~ James M. Kouzes
> & Barry Z. Posner,
> *The Leadership Challenge*

CHALLENGING THE STATUS QUO is tough for many people who do not want to rock the boat. Many people think mediocrity is okay. It might be a personality thing, but do you really think Steve Jobs built Apple with mediocrity? Do you really think Mark Zuckerberg built Facebook with mediocrity? Look at the founders of Instagram, LinkedIn, Method, Amazon, Virgin, or Tesla. Did they think mediocrity was okay? No, they did not, and they changed the world as we know it. I do not think Elon Musk would say, "I wake up every day to meet the status quo and achieve mediocrity." Not every team has to have the mentality of Elon Musk, Steve Jobs, or Jeff Bezos, but challenging the status quo and expecting that mentality from the leaders of your team can lend itself to new and fresh ideas for moving the business forward.

Challenging the status quo requires thinking differently than the way you used to think. Albert Einstein said, "We cannot solve our problems with the same level of thinking that created them."[1] During my time in the military, I learned about military strategy. One strategy was to ensure the team had the "high ground" on the enemy. In war, the high ground has a lot of advantages; wider fields of fire, better cover and concealment, better knowledge of the enemy, better understanding of the enemy situation. I remember while I was in Army training playing the enemy (Op4) and I was trying to climb a mountain with my weapon while attempting to outflank my enemy on the top of the hill. It was extremely difficult. The opposition saw me before I saw them. While trying to advance up the mountain, I kept looking up and trying not to trip on everything in front of me. I tried to communicate with the soldiers on my team, but everything about our situation was at a disadvantage. To me, this scenario exhibits a good visual of what it might look like to challenge the status quo and think about a problem from a different angle—the high ground.

OUTSIDE THE BOX: LEADERS STRUGGLING TO THINK DIFFERENTLY
As the Eagles bounced between the Norming and Performing Stages of team building, I realized the leaders needed to start thinking differently about problems. Many of the leaders struggled to challenge the status quo. They were empowered, but many of them never had to exhibit those skills in the past, so it was uncomfortable for them. I decided to hold another All Leader Meeting to teach why elevating the thinking is important to the growth of the team.

Taking from my experience in the Army, I showed a slide with soldiers on the top of a hill and the enemy at the bottom of the hill. I included the Einstein quote on levels of thinking at the beginning of the presentation and painted a picture of why thinking about a problem at a higher level can provide an advantage. I walked the leaders through the learnings from the military high-ground strategy. In the slide with the hill, I explained how the soldiers at the top of the hill had a competitive advantage over the soldiers at the bottom of the hill because they had the following information:

- The size of the enemy army below

- The avenues of approach the army below could take in order to get to the top of the hill

- The weather

- The type of weapons they have

- Better cover and concealment

Of course, most of my leaders had not been in the military so it was important for me to provide examples as to how having the high ground (thinking about problems from a different level) works in an operational and business environment. A common problem that occurred within the team, as well as in other teams in the company, was increased overtime hours for team members in order to accomplish a higher volume of freight entering the building during peak seasons. I asked my team members how we should solve the problem of overtime. The answer I got from leaders and other team members was, "It is impossible, Patrick. The workload is too much to accomplish within the 40-hour standard."

Overtime is a problem for many reasons. The hourly team members like it because they get extra money (that is a good thing), but this means they take time away from their families. Fatigue sets in over long hours, creating potential for injuries, quality mistakes, and low performance. Think about sports—what happens when a college football team goes into four over-times? The players are tired, make mistakes they do not typically make, and are prone to cramping and injuries. There is a reason the government regulates the number of hours an employee can work before the company must pay overtime wages.

Now, from a business standpoint, overtime can cost thousands of un-planned dollars within the P&L. My leaders, including some senior exec-utives, would tell me, "Patrick, we have to service our customers. We have to take care of the community. Overtime is a necessity to ensure we take care of our stores." I did not disagree with them, but there had to be a better way to think about the problem. For example, what if the team planned to use 100 hours of strategic overtime for $1,000 versus an uncontrolled 1,000 hours of unplanned overtime for $50,000? That is a significant difference to the business P&L.

During this All Leader Meeting, I used the same bullet points as in the military example and tied it to the problem of overtime.

- The size of the army below
  - The team had the tools to figure out during which shifts most of the volume of freight would enter the building. It would not be an even split of cases entering the building on all four shifts.

- The weather
  - The team had a calendar of which team members had vacation during this holiday season. The leaders also knew which team members traditionally skipped work during the holidays.
  - The leaders also knew which team members had flexibility to adjust their shifts for a short time period.

- The type of weapons the army below has.
  - The teams knew how to predict which type of equipment was essential to ensure a smooth, efficient operation. The maintenance team had the ability to prioritize certain equipment for specific times during the operation.

- Better cover and concealment
  - The team had the luxury of planning out in advance all overtime that would be required in a worst-case scenario.

The example above was actually executed and saved the team, building, and company a lot of wasted time and money. It helped by this point that the team was close to the Performing Stage and beginning to believe in the vision.

We could have maintained our existing mentality of just getting through the day and doing whatever it took to service the customers. But we had become a high-performing team that was able to challenge the status quo, to challenge the old ways of thinking. Yes, some hourly team members were unhappy that they did not make as much overtime as they had in previous peak events. However, they were much less so because the leaders and I put together a communication plan well in advance to inform the hourly team members of our approach, and most importantly, we explained the "why" behind the decision.

I can honestly say that the Eagles entered the Performing Stage for good not too long after this meeting. Of course, there was a lot of "inspecting what you expect" and follow up with the team, but the leaders began thinking differently about the business. The Performing Stage is a stage every team wants to stay in once they reach it, but the team needs to understand that you must continue to raise your thinking, challenge the status quo, and strive for perfection. As Vince Lombardi so eloquently put it, "Perfection is not attainable, but if we chase perfection, we can catch excellence."[2] This is how you stay ahead of the competition. You are never really "there." You never really make it, especially because leaders move on, especially in a "leadership factory," which is why the Playbook and the Back-to-Basics Standard Operating Procedure were the foundational element and key to success, respectively. It is why being "Excellent in the Ordinary"[3] is what makes or breaks a team, regardless of size or operational complexity.

TRAJECTORY: THE S-CURVE OF LEARNING

I like to compare the learning "S" curve with challenging the status quo. As Andy Stanley says, "Leaders' IQ goes down [sic] the longer they are in an organization. They are the least aware of their own culture because they grow blind to the problems in front of them. They become painters who never smell the paint."[4] This is why it is important to have fresh eyes and bring in new talent from outside the organization and also to make sure you do not have leaders in the same role for too long. They become too comfortable. The S-curve of learning follows a learner's journey from unfamiliarity to mastery.[5] According to Wikipedia, a learning curve is a graphical representation of the relationship between how proficient someone is at a task and the amount of experience they have. Proficiency (measured on the vertical axis) usually increases with increased experience (the horizontal axis); that is to say, the more someone performs a task, the better they get at it.[6]

When someone joins a team or starts a new role, they start at the bottom of the S-curve. It will take them six to nine months to truly understand the job they are performing. Then, they will start to do well in the role and begin to make an impact on the business. After about two or three years of performing the same role, the tasks performed in the role become second nature, the speed in which they see the business slows down, and this is the "sweet spot" for this person. They are a "go-to person" on the team. However, if an individual is in the same role for too long, he/she becomes complacent and his/her performance will level off and/or start to decline, which is the top of the S-curve. There are a few things that can occur with leaders at the top of their S-curve.

1. They choose to stay in that role because it is familiar and comfortable. They do not want to rock the boat, so they stop challenging the status quo and moving the business forward.

2. Their organization chooses to keep them in the same role because there is comfort with having a good worker in a role that does not require any hiring. After all, training another person would take time and money, none of which the organization wants to deal with.

3. They disrupt themselves by jumping to a new S-curve, which is explained well in the book *Disrupt Yourself: Putting the Power of Disruptive Innovation to Work* written by Whitney Johnson. They realize the best way to learn and grow is to build their experience with other roles and responsibilities. This is where the different level of thinking occurs.

In the quote at the beginning of the chapter from *The Leadership Challenge*, James M. Kouzes & Barry Z. Posner says, "Leaders must challenge the process. Precisely, because any system will unconsciously conspire to maintain the status quo and prevent change." This is why I think the learning S-curve is related to challenging the status quo within an organization. If the top executives in an organization have been in the same role for seven years or more, this is a dangerous place to be. It is difficult to think about the business differently when you have been running the same process every day or speaking about the same things for that long. And if that is the mentality at the executive level, then there are chances the mid-level leaders and teammates have been in their roles for too long as well. An organization is able to challenge the status quo and think differently when they are bringing in fresh, new ideas on a consistent basis. It doesn't necessarily have to be from outside the company, but that does not hurt. There are many examples of a company running the same processes for years, and they bring in a talent from the outside, who–within a few times of using the process–makes a suggestion to improve it, which saves the company time and money.

CHALLENGING THE STATUS QUO IS HARD

My career at the company progressed because I was an "outsider" willing to think differently and question the processes that were in place. The processes that made the company great were appropriate for the time in which they were created, but processes are meant to change. I can say for certain that since I left, the company has done a great job of pivoting and changing their processes while maintaining its strong culture.

Challenging the status quo is not always easy or popular. There is risk involved for sure, and it takes courage to keep thinking differently when it seems like everyone is pushing against you. Glenn Llopis wrote an article in Forbes called "Five Reasons Leaders are Afraid to Challenge the Status Quo." He says, "Status quo is defined as preserving the existing state of affairs. It's about doing what is comfortable and thinking inside the existing box. This is so much easier than being uncomfortable and thinking outside the box or that the box is bigger than you ever imagined. It is also easier than thinking you might not be thinking in the right boxes anymore to recreate growth." Glen Llopis outlines the following reasons leaders do not challenge the status quo.

1. They're unwilling to turn the spotlight of accountability on themselves

2. They're afraid of risk

3. They don't know how to get started

4. They lack organizational readiness

5. They have not evolved as leaders

Of the five reasons, I personally think "risk" is the main reason leaders do not challenge the status quo. Thinking differently requires change, and change is really hard. That is why there are change management professionals and hundreds of books written about it. Risk also involves potential for failure which can be scary for job stability. If you are leading correctly, you are empowering your team members to make decisions, and if you are encouraging them to think outside the box and challenge the old ways of thinking, then, yes, there is a lot of unpredictable risk, but also benefit involved. You do not know what decisions they will make, but this is where ownership in their development comes into play.

John Wooden, legendary UCLA basketball coach, says, "Big things are accomplished only through the perfection of minor details." By this point in the book, you've learned about building trust and credibility, developing structure, and putting it all together. You have heard me talk about having the discipline to do the little things right every time, which is what Coach Wooden is talking about. As you build your team and go through transition phases of team development, the empowerment and trust you have in your team to execute the things you taught them increases, which means the "risk" level decreases. Will there be times when your team makes the wrong decision about which status quo to challenge? Yes, absolutely. And when the wrong decision is made, you take ownership of it but still encourage them to keep thinking differently.

WHAT WOULD FUNDAMENTALLY CHANGE THE BUSINESS?

I heard this quote in a podcast when I was leading the Eagles, "Ask yourself: What do I believe is impossible to do in my field, but if it could be done, would fundamentally change everything."[7] I have to believe this is what Steve Jobs and Elon Musk thought about daily when developing their companies. It does not have to be a cancer-curing idea or a flying-to-Mars idea, but it must challenge the old ways of thinking. I do not know how many times in my career (and your career I am sure) I heard someone say, "Do not waste your time, that is impossible." There was a point in time when touching your finger to a screen to know anything you wanted to know was considered impossible until the smartphone was developed. Imagine if Apple said, "That is impossible, why try?" They would never have developed the iPhone. Innovators at Apple looked at the world, and said, "What do I believe to be impossible, but if I could develop it, would fundamentally change my business?" They have created hundreds of products people love because they "think differently."

This question was posed to the Eagles team during the Performing Stage of the journey. By this time, the team was extremely efficient and examined and improved the easier "low hanging fruit" within the operation. When I asked the question, "Team, we have made so many great strides with safety, culture, development, and operational performance. What can we do to improve it further in order to better serve our team members and customers? What is something that our competitors are not doing? What is something other distribution centers within the company in the country are not doing?"

One area of the business that caught our eye was shipping. The shipping process was pretty standard. There was a group of individuals who drove battery-operated pallet jacks to stack cases seven feet tall. In operations, these individuals are called orderfillers. Each individual wore a headset and received instructions from a computer voice about which product to pick up. Each pallet the orderfiller stacked was designed for a specific store in the region. The orderfiller dropped the pallets off at a big wrap machine. There were several team members on mechanical pallet jacks, called wrappers, who wrapped the pallets and staged the wrapped pallets in front of a loading dock. Then, there were loaders who put all the wrapped pallets onto the empty trailer.

It always seemed like there were inefficiencies within this process and a lot of opportunities to damage the product or make a mistake. The leaders examined this existing process–which was conducted in 40 other distribution centers across the country–to fundamentally change the business by thinking differently. The team explored what it might look like if the orderfillers wrapped their own pallets at the wrap machine and then staged them at the dock door. If this adjustment proved actionable, this could save the company a significant number of labor hours. The goal was to eliminate the wrapper function, but not eliminate jobs of the team members. Team members always fear change from what they are familiar with. They asked whether or not the wrapper and loader jobs would be eliminated, because that had occurred in the past with the introduction of new technology. This is a legitimate fear and one that a leader must be cognizant of and have empathy toward. This is why I emphasized with the team that the intent of the new process and technique was not to reduce the workforce, but to shift them to other areas of the business where they could be better utilized.

The leaders in the building did not just come up with the idea and implement it. The leaders met with the hourly team members who would be impacted and informed them of the pilot program. We explained the purpose behind the new program and initiative. We explained the "why" and how it would impact them. We did not hide anything. We were not trying to be sneaky. We wanted them to be a part of the journey and part of the solution. I brought in an engineer to ensure the standards set forth for the orderfillers were fair and consistent. We tested the program on one group within the building before expanding it to other areas of the building and other shifts.

Once the standard was set, the pilot program proved successful, and all team members who were previously working as wrappers had new roles on the team. Then, we developed the new standard operating procedure to add to our Playbook. From ideation to execution, it took nearly six months. This process improved operational efficiency by 5%, increased quality, decreased the number of damaged cases, and actually improved safety within the building.

The leaders had built trust and credibility by this time with the hourly team members so they believed us when we said there would be no jobs eliminated. The team understood the vision and goals for the year. They understood how the structure was put in place to help each individual be the best version of themselves at work. The standard operating procedure we developed was sent to other buildings within the company to help improve their operation.

A NEW LENS: LEADER'S PERSPECTIVE

During the process of writing this book and a few years after I left the team, I spent some time asking some of the leaders how the cultural turnaround took place from their perspective. A few of them mentioned a "stagnant culture" unable to get out of old habits. They talked about how hourly team members could not make decisions without a manager present, and how there was a lack of accountability for results. They mentioned that the company was comfortable in the supply chain because they helped revolutionize it, but then competitors came along and disrupted everything. Team members employed by the company for a long time only knew one way to do things and therefore thought it was the best way. The thought of having to change truly scared them. I mean, think about it: if they believed they had been doing it the best way for 50 years, how could there possibly be a different, better way of managing a supply chain? This is what the leaders meant by a stagnant culture.

Prior to my arrival, other leaders had come into the building several times to "fix it." They came into this stagnant, resistant culture and they tried to "strongarm the change." These leaders from the outside tried to tell the leaders who had been there for 15 years, "You do not know what you are doing. Your approach is not working." The advice given to the managers by the outside leaders was to do whatever was necessary to make the hourly team members happy. One of the many problems with this approach is that—in my experience—90% of the complaints and issues come from 10% of the team members. I used to tell my leaders that I spend 90% of my time with the 10% of the team who probably should not be on the team in the first place because of their attitudes. That leaves only 10% of my time to spend on the 90% of the team who come into work every day to give their best. Doing whatever the hourly team member wants in order to keep them happy means that a leader would mainly be listening to the 10% who most likely have only their own personal interests in mind. They are not trying to make things better for the team, they are trying to make things better for themselves.

My approach was obviously very different. I was not perfect by any means, but I stuck to my process and believed I had the best interest of the team in mind. The leaders I spoke to after I left said, "Today, the hourly team members are close to being able to run the building themselves." I asked them why they thought that. They answered that it was "because of the structure now in place and the confidence everyone now has in themselves." I never viewed challenging the status quo as a way to build confidence until I spoke to the leaders, but they explained:

> *The expectations put in place through the structure and SOPs set an expectation. Team members were rewarded for thinking differently. If an individual did not follow the processes in place, they were held accountable and began to feel like an outsider. When leaders got out of their comfort zone and believed the work they did had value, their confidence increased. As their confidence in-*

creased, their 'buy' into the vision and process increased as well. They became better leaders, and also better humans. It became contagious to say, 'We can solve this problem if we can think about it differently.[8]

KAIZEN: CONTINUOUS IMPROVEMENT

In my career, 1 was fortunate to learn about Lean Six Sigma, Kaizen, 5S, and Continuous Improvement (CI), among other things. This gave me a certain mindset that, coupled with my military experience, melded to effectively build high-performing teams. I was never going to be a master at any of them, but each provided skills for my leadership tool kit. The thing I believe to be valuable with Kaizen (continuous improvement) is that it is closely related to challenging the status quo. The very essence of wanting to improve a process by eliminating waste is to challenge the current state of that process. Kaizen is not just about operational processes. It is about the elimination of waste; it is about providing different structures to multiple areas of the business. It might involve reducing the time it takes for a case of meat to get from one end of a distribution center to the other. It might mean reducing the number of reports a finance analyst has to send to the business partners in a week. It could be the consolidation of meetings to free up time to do actual work, or it could be a decrease in the time it takes to launch a new product. Whatever area of business you are in, there are improvements that can make the processes more efficient.

As a leader, you cannot start trying to improve the processes within the team until you understand the baseline of the current process. It would not be a good idea within your first few days of joining a team to start changing the existing processes your team has used for years. Remember, trust and credibility are where you start every time. As you move through the four stages of team development, you will encounter an appropriate time to improve processes. Perhaps it is when you are implementing structure and organization within the team. Perhaps it's when you are creating your "leadership factory" and creating effective development programs. Either way, when you are in the Performing and Norming Stages, Kaizen is a great method to use to challenge the status quo and get your team to think differently about the problems it faces.

As you deep dive into the team and understand more clearly the current process, then it is time to challenge that process. This is where using Kaizen techniques can be useful. Involve your team members in the discussion. Each team member knows the process much better than you do, so listen to what he/she has to say. This continuous improvement process is something you do with the team, NOT to the team.[9] As waste is eliminated, the team will become more efficient. Team morale will improve as team members see the impact. The mindset of the team will shift in a positive way. Team members will begin to see the benefit of challenging the way processes were conducted in the past. Whether this shift in mindset occurs in the middle of the team transformation, or at the end, the result is an organization that wants to learn and improve each day in order to help the overall team get one step closer to achieving its vision.

How can my company challenge the status quo?

Remember, this book is about providing a real-life example on how to transform a team using proven team-building principles. The Eagles are a real operational team that endured this process, but please look to understand how you can apply these concepts and principles to your finance, marketing, procurement, or engineering team. Despite what business sector you are in, in every team, a leader will struggle with getting individuals to think differently about the problems they face. Teams will look at how they solved problems in the past. That is not necessarily a bad thing because chances are, the problems will still get solved; however, then the question becomes, "Are you elevating the business? Are you moving the business forward?" In times of crisis or challenging times, the teams that turn the crisis into opportunity are the teams that win in the long-term. You cannot turn a crisis into a positive opportunity for gain if you are only solving problems as they come up and only thinking about the business in the same way you have always thought about it.

Empower your teams to examine what the competitors are doing well and what the unmet needs of the consumer are. For instance, if you are leading a marketing team, have you just modified your same "staple" product over the past five years hoping the consumer will not pick up on the fact that it is the same product, tweaked slightly with minor differentiating features? What would happen if you asked your team members to develop a feature on the product that is considered impossible, but would fundamentally change the product and the lives of the consumers who use it? It would be difficult for your team to respond to that challenge by thinking and behaving the way they have always thought and done.

You could also spend time with your engineers in a brainstorming session as they talk about different products to bring to the market. Listen to the attitude and tone in the room. What do you hear? Do you hear them saying:

"That is just not possible."

"It would cost too much."

"It is too complex and we do not have the resources."

All of these are fair comments, but this shows that the team is not willing to dream. They are not willing to take chances. They are afraid to fail. They are limiting their ability to challenge the status quo. When building a team, the leader should encourage team members to think outside the box and think differently about the business and problems that occur in order to solve them. There was a time when using a smartphone was considered impossible. There was a time when driving from one end of the country to the other without gasoline was considered impossible. Just because the solution is not directly in front of your face, does not mean there is not a way to make something possible.

KEY TAKEAWAYS OF CHAPTER 8:

1. Challenging the status quo requires team members to think differently from the way they are used to thinking.

2. The team must be excellent in the ordinary before they can begin to challenge the status quo.

3. The S-curve of learning is a way of thinking to reduce complacency and challenge the status quo to make yourself and others around you better.

4. Challenging the status quo is hard. Sometimes you will feel like you are on an island by yourself trying to get others to buy into alternative ways of looking at current problems.

5. Ask yourself: "What do I believe is impossible to do in my field, but if it could be done, would fundamentally change everything?"

Chapter Nine:

100% Ownership at All Levels

"Responsibility equals accountability equals ownership. And a sense of ownership is the most powerful weapon a team or organization can have."

~ Pat Summitt

CREATING A CULTURE OF 100% ownership at all levels is not something that happens overnight. This occurs very deep into the four stages of team development when the team spends more time in the Performing Stage, and as the team directs their energy into learning and improving daily in order to achieve the goals set forth. It is one thing to have a few leaders taking ownership of the actions and behaviors of the team. It is another when every level of the team takes 100% ownership. Much of what I am going to discuss next comes from Jocko Willink, a former Navy Seal and co-author of *Extreme Ownership*. As I was leading my team and executing the Playbook, I began listening to his podcast and reading his book.

My team was struggling to put it all together. We were struggling to get out of the Norming Phase and be fully into the Performing Stage. This was 100% my fault. I could not convince the leaders and team to buy into the vision 100% even though we had seen great success. The team seemed to be satisfied with meeting our goals; I wanted to exceed the goals and continue to get better and better. I wanted the team to be excellent in the ordinary and perform the little things correctly every day. I believed the best way to obtain long-term results was to not focus on short-term gains. Decisions were made with the vision in mind; I was playing the long game in order to promote a sustainable culture.

Simon Sinek's book *The Infinite Game* did not come out until after I left, so I did not have the benefit of his wisdom, but this was my attempt at 100% ownership. Even before Sinek's book, I was talking about being in the game for the long haul, not treating business like a finite game where there is a winner and a loser or a beginning, middle, and end. When every team member believes in the vision, and takes ownership of his/her actions, then it does not matter who the leader is or what the short-term goal is, the team engages in an infinite game and mindset.[1]

WHERE YOU FIT IN: MAKE THE CONNECTION TO WHO YOU ARE
After two-and-a-half years, the team was just beginning to dip into the Performing Stage. I was walking the floor of the operation, and stopped to talk to one of my Area Leaders, which is something I did on a daily basis. He and I started talking about leadership, which fires me up; I could talk for days to a listening ear and teachable leader. The Area Leader stopped me mid-sentence and said, "You know Patrick, you are thinking so far ahead of all of us at all times that most of us struggle to catch up. As a result, some just give up. I am not saying that is a bad thing, but some, including me, do not know how to connect with you because we do not understand how you think." This stopped me dead in my tracks. In my heart I believed that I came to work every day for the team. I know what is best for the team. I love this team. I would do anything for anyone on the team because I believe in them, but I missed out big on what they needed. I was talking AT them, not WITH them.

A few days after the conversation with the Area Leader, I was running before work, listening to Jocko's podcast when he interviewed Brian Stann, who was a UFC fighter and Marine Commander in Iraq. I was actually caught off guard by how much this interview spoke to everything I was trying to teach my own team. Brian played football at the United States Naval Academy and had a similar military career to mine. With regard to standards and discipline, he says, "You are either meeting the expectation or you are not. There is no in between and it is nothing personal." So many times teammates think a leader takes things personally when the teammate is held accountable. This is simply not true.

Brian also discussed the importance of discipline. He told a story of when he was leading Marines in combat, and was especially hard on them about doing the little things right like following the SOPs in place. One day in Iraq, it was 100 degrees out and he made his Marines wear their kevlar helmets and body armor all day because of the protection it provided. Yes, it was hot and the easy thing to do was to take the equipment off to cool down, but this could expose them to danger from the enemy. A Marine gunman who had held his position behind a wall for several hours peeked into a hole (disregarding standard procedure) and exposed himself for a split second to catch a cool breeze. This moment of poor discipline cost the Marine his life. The Marine was shot by an enemy sniper and killed. In the military, lack of discipline could mean losing a life or the life of another. You had better believe this type of thinking translates into business. Maybe lives are not on the line, but millions of dollars and the families of those you lead and serve are impacted when you lack discipline.

Jocko, then, went on to explain taking ownership over team failures using a failed military mission as an example. This especially resonated with me after my conversation with the Area Leader about the team struggling to connect with my approach to leadership. I listened to this podcast three more times and decided I knew what the right approach would be for my team. I was going to borrow elements of this conversation to let my team know who I was and why I thought the way I did. I put together a presentation for the monthly All Leader Meeting.

SUCCESS VS. FAILURE: THE OWNERSHIP PRESENTATION

For this All Leader Meeting with 60 teammates, I waited until everyone was seated and eating lunch, then I asked questions surrounding success and failure. I explained that success and failure are different for every individual and every team. Success is defined by whether you achieved your true potential, which is something I learned from Coach John Wooden. I tied this to operational performance which, in a distribution center, is measured by cases per man hour (CPH). It is the measure of how many cases the team can get in and out of the building during a time period/given day. A standard building like mine would have a 185 CPH Goal. I told the team,

> *If your goal set by the company was to achieve 185 cases per man hour, but you had the potential to move 190 CPH, and you only achieved 187 cases per man hour this would be a miss and a failure. In the eyes of the company, you achieved your goal, but true success is achieving your potential. On the contrary, if the goal set by the company was to achieve 185 cases per man hour, but your team was only capable of achieving 180 cases per man hour, and you achieved 183 cases per man hour, this would be a success. The company does not determine your success; you, as the leaders of the team do. This does not mean you set your sights low and under-promise and overachieve. You should evaluate your team based upon data.*

I transitioned into asking more questions of the leaders. I put a line down the middle of the screen and on the left side of the presentation, I listed several failures of the team. I asked who owned the failure of the housekeeping walk conducted by the Senior Vice President of the Company? A few leaders raised their hands and said, "Patrick, I own that one." I asked who owns the poor communication to our hourly teammates? A few leaders again raised their hands saying they owned it. I asked who owned the high turnover in the building, lack of ownership at all levels, and the individuals not following the SOPs in place that caused the team to be out of balance. Many of the leaders took ownership of these failures. I appreciated the level of ownership some of my leaders took because it showed progress in the way the team thought. Next, on the right side of the slides I made a list of all the successes on the team. I asked the team who owned the consistent high performance of the building, high hourly team member incentive, success of the P&L, the fact that the team had one of the safest teams in the country? There were crickets in the room.

Lastly, I said, "Who owns these successes and failures of the team?" On the left side I put a box around the failures and put my name at the top of it, and then I put a box around the successes and put the Eagles Leaders above it. I explained,

> *I appreciate all of you who took ownership of the failures, but those failures are mine. As the leader of this amazing team, I answer to those failures, and I am happy to do so. You, as the Eagles Leaders, own the successes. I could never accomplish on my own what you all have accomplished. This is truly how I think and what I believe.*

This is what ownership looks like. As a leader, the reason I own the mistakes/failures is because I did not train the leaders well enough. I did not put enough effort into getting "buy in" from the team. I did not teach the team well enough to understand the Playbook, the SOPs, the standards, or how to perform their jobs. This concept and way of living does not just apply in business. It applies in all aspects of life. If your marriage fails, you have ownership in your actions that caused your partner to lose trust in the relationship. You own your relationship. If you lose touch with your friends from college, you own the reasons why you are not close anymore. If you live an unhealthy lifestyle, you own your actions as to why you are unhealthy. Making excuses does nothing for you.

OWNERSHIP	
PATRICK	**EAGLES LEADERS**
1. Housekeeping failure: 　　a. Who owns this?	1. 6 week trend of 180+ CPH 　(performance) 　　　a. Who owns this?
2. Poor communication 　between teams 　　a. Who owns this?	2. $.90 Hourly team 　incentive (highest ever) 　　　a. Who owns this?
3. Specific job functions 　below 100% performance 　　a. Who owns this?	3. 12 of 13 lines on P&L 　made (1st time ever) 　　　a. Who owns this?
4. 46% Team turnover 　　a. Who owns this?	4. Top 5 safest teams in 　company 　　　a. Who owns this?
5. Lack of ownership by team 　　a. Who owns this?	

Next, I took the meeting into the concept of expectations. I said (borrowing from Brian Stann), "There is an expectation, and you are either meeting the expectation or you are not. There is no in between. Some of you might not understand what that looks like, so let me show you." By this time in the journey, the standards were set and clear. The Playbook was in full effect. The SOPs had been rolled out and communicated, and there were clear expectations regarding everything the leaders and team did. Every leader and team member knew what they would be held accountable for, which tied to the vision and goals set forth. We started February 1 (Day One) of the company's new year by setting a very clear initial expectation. Everyone knew on Day One what was expected of them for the next 364 days of the year. The next slide I showed was a line with the words "Expectation Line" on it. Above it was phrases around a certain mentality I communicated to the team over and over again; 100% effort, committed to the vision and team, thinking differently, and taking ownership. Below the line were manager-type mentalities such as just getting through the day, missing goals with little effort of changing, and not taking ownership.

EXPECTATIONS

1. It's about meeting the expectations set forth. The standards are clear. If they are not clear to you, then you need to speak up

2. There is meeting the expectation. And there is not meeting it. The line is drawn at meeting it.

---

1. 100% effort

2. Committed to the vision & Eagles

3. Think differently and challenge the status quo

4. Willing to make a mistake to move the business forward

5. Taking ownership of the operations—Holding team members to the expectation

EXPECTATION LINE

1. Clock in / Clock out Mentality

2. Miss goals with zero effort to change

3. Not following the directions/guidance/SOPs/Playbook in place

4. Not setting up your team for success

5. Not taking ownership—Ghosting and not holding team members to the standard

I took the leaders through a rollercoaster of emotions up until this point. Then, I transitioned the conversation. This is what I said:

> *This team has made significant progress over the past 18 months. You have taken a leap of faith, but we are not done yet. I believe we have reached a crossroad. Some of you are struggling to dive fully in and be 100% committed to the vision and goals we set forth. Over the past several weeks, I have tried to put myself in your shoes and understand your struggles from your perspective. If I am you, I am thinking, I have been here for 15 years at this building, making it work. Sure, we are not perfect, but who does this guy think he is? His military approach will not work here in this atmosphere. I realized, although I teach about being transparent, some of you probably do not truly understand my approach or who I am. What makes Patrick tick? Why is he the way he is? Why is he obsessed with the minor details? Why is he so hard on us? Talking to you about my reasons is not going to move the needle. I came across this conversation on the Jocko Podcast that I believe explains it better than I ever can. The clip I am going to share with you is only 15 minutes; I spliced together the conversations within the two-and-a-half-hour podcast that are relevant to the Eagles. The conversation is between Brian Stann, who is a UFC Fighter and former Marine Platoon Commander, and Jocko Willink, a former Naval Seal Commander.*

After I played the clip, I asked the leaders what stood out to them. Several of them talked about different elements, but they got a much better understanding of who I was, why I taught the things I taught, and that I truly cared about the success of the team. I explained that my approach was to hold nothing personal toward anyone and that there are no lives on the line because there are no bullets flying. With that being said, I explained to the team that I was afraid if we took our foot off the pedal now, we might take steps back in our progress, impacting the lives of everyone the team had worked so hard to influence. If there was a slowdown in progress, and the team reverted back to its old ways, then the team members who trusted us, would likely lose sight of the vision. This could result in poor safety again. Morale would also decline due to working longer hours, spending more time away from family, and missing out on money through the performance incentive.

I ended the meeting with a story about a team member who I had recently spoken with on the operational floor. After spending about 10 minutes with the team member, one of my mid-level leaders approached the team member. The hourly team member asked the leader what his thoughts were about me (Patrick) as a leader.

Team member: "Patrick seems tough and a no-nonsense type of person."

My leader: "Patrick cares about standards and disciplines and doing the little things right. He cares about taking care of the team, and holds a high standard of excellence."

Team member: "Whatever that guy has done, he has put more money in my pocket through the performance incentive and efficiency within the team than any other leader to come to the building. My family owes him a lot."

My leader: "That is true, his plan is truly working."

You might be thinking I am patting myself on the back. I am puffing out my chest and feeling pretty good about the work I accomplished. This could not be further from the truth. This was disheartening to hear. From an ownership perspective, I failed to effectively communicate and influence the whole team so they understood who the real heroes of the cultural turnaround were. This was not a good response. I told the leaders that this team member totally missed it, but it was not his fault. The message around the team is that I was the savior. I came to fix this team and I did just that. I explained:

There is no way I could have done anything without everyone on the team. I did not put a dime in that team member's pocket. I did not run the operation. I was not the one who made the building safe. I am getting credit for all of your hard work. This will happen and did happen when the team does not take 100% ownership of the vision and goals set forth. Sure, there are tough conversations to be had, but when team members and leaders say 'Patrick said . . . ,' this is a determinant and JV leadership as Brian Stann and Jocko would say. This undermines your authority and leadership in the eyes of the team member. Our team members are not your friends. You are their leader. It is your job to take care of them. You take care of them through discipline and enforcing the standard. You take care of them by taking 100% ownership of the bad and praising them for the good.

FINAL THOUGHTS

1. What stood out to you?
   a. Leader factory, the expectation line. Discipline; So afraid of going back to $.05 incentive (not coming home); the hourly team members are not your friends (dichotomy of leadership); Leadership appearance (Personal Brand); empowerment of leaders/team members)
2. Hopefully this gives you a better idea of who Patrick is, where I come from, and why failure to meet expectations will not be tolerated. I know you are not used to this, and for that, I HAVE to amp up my teaching.
3. Know this, I want nothing but to see each of you succeed, and the Eagles to reach their FULL POTENTIAL. If you believe I have a different agenda, then I'm not communicating effectively.
4. Lastly- JV Leadership: take ownership of decisions

EAGLES FLY TOGETHER

OWNERSHIP MANTRA: SEE IT. OWN IT. FIX IT.

One way you can teach your team 100% ownership is by pushing the mantra "See It, Own It, Fix It." This is a concept I took from *The Oz Principle* and modified to work for my team. During your journey through the four stages of team development, you will have many frustrations, and you will see things from a different lens than your team. You will attempt to connect the dots, which sometimes just confuses them more. I found myself in this frustrating realm of trying to get my hourly team members and leaders to take ownership of his/her actions, and those of the team. Eventually, it just happened that I repeated myself over and over again: See It, Own It, Fix It. *The Oz Principle* examines the role of accountability in the achievement of business results and the improvement of both individual and organizational performance. It presents an approach where an employee makes "a personal choice to rise above [her/his] circumstances and demonstrate the ownership necessary for achieving desired results to See It, Own It, Solve It, and Do It."[2]

I applied it to my leaders and team members by saying, when you See something that is not correct, you take Ownership of it, and Fix it. If team members see another team member not following the standards set forth such as creating a safety issue, they must take ownership of what they witnessed, address it with the other team member, and follow up with him/her to ensure it does not happen again. If a team member sees an item out of place (in the 5S set up) such as a broom left lying in the aisle or on the ground, he/she should not walk past it and "hope" someone else fixes it. He/she must take the ownership of that broom, and place (fix) the broom back where it belongs.

Before the team had bought in 100% and had 100% ownership at all levels (during the Storming Phase), I would get frustrated with leaders and teammates making a comment like, "Patrick, it's a broom. Why does it matter? Is this broom going to get us to perform better? Your obsession with the brooms is ridiculous." What the team soon began to understand is that the brooms represented standards and discipline. The brooms represented dedication to the vision and goals. It represented the mentality of the whole team. The brooms represented the balance within the building and the ownership of the team. The brooms were something everyone on the team and in the building saw on a consistent basis that represented bigger elements of the business and indicated whether or not the team was properly focused on the bigger goals. If the team could not take care of the little things within the operation, then there was no way they were performing the bigger tasks to standard.

According to the Broken Window Theory, visible signs of crime, anti-social behavior, and civil disorder create an urban environment that encourages further crime and disorder, including serious crimes.[3] This has been applied to business as well, and it was a theory I taught to my team. It applies to the brooms, 5S, housekeeping, and doing the little things right. When a broom is out of place and lying on the ground versus hanging in its correct spot, other team members see that and they think it's okay to walk past trash that they normally might pick up. They think to themselves, "Others are not putting the broom away, or cleaning when they walk past trash, so this must not be important anymore." This little lack of discipline leads to bigger discipline problems like not handing the shift over to the next team properly, or not stopping a forklift at the end of an aisle, which could lead to someone getting seriously injured. This is why connecting this theory with the concept of See It, Own It, Fix It is critical. Even if there are a few individuals who take a shortcut on disciplined tasks, there are other teammates who will address what they see before it becomes a bigger deal and has a larger impact on the team.

The "Teachable Moment" I discussed earlier in this Chapter did not and could not have occurred early in the four stages of team development. Teaching your team ownership is something that happens throughout the whole process from start to finish, but will need to be something you are thinking about on Day One. While you follow the guidance given in the beginning chapters of this book, you begin to plant the seed for your team to take ownership. As I saw the shift in ownership in the Eagles, and the team got to a good point in the journey where they understood the importance, I developed an SOP that assigned equal ownership to different projects and initiatives we agreed to take on at the beginning of the year in order to think differently and move the business forward. The different projects and initiatives focused on safety, operational efficiencies, housekeeping, development, and structure. All these helped move the team toward the vision by putting us in the best position to achieve the goals set forth. A chart from the SOP is included here.

Eagles Projects / Initiatives / Ownership
The below leaders will be responsible for the successful implementation of the project or initiative

Project	Details
Floor Scrubber Schedule	Design a schedule for scrubber to operate 24/7
Light on Docks	Fix/update all the lights on the receiving/shipping docks
Air Compressor on Shipping Dock	Install an Air Compressor at 50% of dock doors to inflate airbags
Gameplan for Success	Plan the whole year in SOP format for all peak seasons, holidays, events, meetings, etc.

Ownership	Details
Cleaning Stations in building	Ensure all cleaning stations are 5Sed & 100% full in whole building
Equipment Parking Plan	Responsible for maintaining all equipment in proper location
Recycle Program	Responsible for ensuring Recycling SOP is followed to standard
Playbook	Responsible for all leaders understanding the Playbook and ensuring all team members are held to same standard

Focus	Owner	Roll out Date
Housekeeping	Leader	Specific Date
Housekeeping	Leader	Specific Date
Efficiency	Leader	Specific Date
Structure	Leader	Specific Date
Focus	**Owner**	**Roll out Date**
Housekeeping	Leader	Specific Date
Structure/Efficiency	Leader	Specific Date
Housekeeping	Leader	Specific Date
Accountability	Leader	Specific Date

You will notice there is clarity around what the program/initiative is, how it applies to the vision, which leader is accountable for it, and the date it should be rolled out. You will also notice it does not tell the leader "How" to achieve the task. The leader is empowered to come up with the best plan and program/initiative by leveraging the resources around them.

BRINGING IT ALL TOGETHER: TYING "WHY" TO OWNERSHIP

When you build trust and credibility, you focus a lot of your time on explaining the "why." In the beginning, there are a lot of questions asked of you as the leader. The team wants to know why you are changing or making adjustments to the way things used to be. They are trying to understand your thought process. They are trying to determine if you are a trustworthy individual. As a result, they want to understand the "why" behind everything. Do not just explain the "what" to your team. If they understand the meaning behind every decision and the reasons why they are asked to perform new tasks, they will be more engaged. If they buy in, they are more likely to take ownership of their actions. Explain how each person's role makes a bigger impact on the team.

For example, many times I had leaders from one shift explain to me that they were not able to complete the tasks necessary to hand the building off properly to the next team because they ran out of time. This, of course, is a lack of ownership and an excuse. I explained many times how their lack of planning and execution impacted the next team in a negative way because I tied it to the big picture. I did not yell at them or tell them they were wrong. I simply explained the "why" behind the task and how their lack of completing the task to standard impacted the next team, and ultimately the whole team, which included their team.

When you, as the leader, begin to talk about vision and goal setting, this will enable the team to start taking ownership. If you came into a team and said, "Team, this is the new vision I came up with for us. I expect you to adhere to it. Here are the goals I am setting for you over the next year. I expect you to adhere to them," I can promise you that your team will resist taking ownership because they do not believe they had any part in the creation of the vision and goals. Help your teammates feel part of something bigger than themselves. In addition, you will need to communicate the vision and goals early and often to keep reminding the team of why you are doing what you are doing. A shared vision and common goals are things all teammates can take ownership of because they helped develop it. Their voices were heard. Their ideas were taken seriously. They were part of the decision-making process that made the vision a reality. Think about the things you personally have taken ownership of in the past, and the things to which you said, "It's not my fault" or "I did not come up with that idea."

As you impose structure and organization, this not only helps explain the "why," but it clearly defines the expectation and provides left and right (guardrails) limits for the team to operate within. When you encourage your team to think outside the box and solve their own problems, they will grow as individuals and be more likely to take ownership of the results. In addition, the structure establishes accountability through clarity around the expectations. You should always trust your leaders and teammates to make sound decisions, yet verify the things you are seeing. This means you need to hold the team accountable for their work, the goals accomplished, and their efforts. Demand 100% effort in all that they do. People who know they will be held accountable for their actions are more likely to take ownership of their actions.

When you, as the leader, witness a teammate taking ownership, it is imperative that you acknowledge this. Praise them. Hail them. And most importantly, do it in front of others. This goes along with how you react when someone thinks outside the box or challenges the status quo. You want to acknowledge this type of thinking and thank the person for his/her courage. This is not the time to yell, berate, or make the person feel inadequate.

DON'T MISS OUT: CONTINUE TO LEARN FROM YOUR TEAM

A great way to get your team to take 100% ownership is to model the way. There are clearly high standards in this approach and process. Earlier in the book, I discussed how I conducted annual evaluations in order to help build trust and credibility. I talked about spending hours preparing and then giving proper feedback to make the leader better. I was tough but fair. No leader walked out of the evaluation without suggestions for improving some area of his/her working life. After I had completed all the annual evaluations, I did something that none of my leaders had seen before; I asked them to evaluate my performance and provide constructive feedback. I gave my 12 leaders two weeks to prepare and evaluate my performance for the year. I had stipulations for my evaluations:

- Each leader had to provide two "sustains" for me.

- Each leader had to provide three "improves" for me.

- No leader could copy the comments of another leader.

- I, as the receiver, was only allowed to ask clarifying questions–no excuses or explanations.

On the day of the evaluation, all 12 leaders came into the conference room where I had three tables lined up in a half circle. In the middle of the half circle was a smaller desk for me to write notes. The leaders sat down in a horseshoe around me. I set the tone for the evaluation by thanking them for the hard work and time put into this process. I explained the intent of the evaluation was for me to grow and be a better leader for the team. I started at one end of the horseshoe and each leader provided his/her sustains and improvements. I wrote notes and listened intently. After about 90 minutes, I had 24 sustains of things I did well and 36 areas to improve. Many of the leaders commented that this was the most difficult task they had ever had to perform because of how awkward it was, but told me that I had made them feel comfortable enough to provide this feedback. After the evaluation, I took a week to type up the notes and digest the feedback. Then, I came up with five areas I was committed to improving the following year. I communicated these areas to the broader team and wrote them on my whiteboard in my office for all to see and where I could review them daily.

I am truly a better leader today because of the positive and constructive feedback my leaders provided to me. I did this all three years on the team. It never got easier, but it became more important than ever as the team transitioned from the Storming phase into the Performing phase. Many of my leaders leveraged this technique with their direct leaders in order to get better, and they saw firsthand the power of a leader taking 100% ownership of his/her actions in front of his/her direct reports, which was impactful to vision buy-in.

RECOGNIZING THE SIGNS: 100% OWNERSHIP AT ALL LEVELS
One hundred percent ownership does not occur because the team members come to work one day and all of a sudden place the team above themselves. Having a vision and goals with a structured team is imperative, but this alone will not influence the team to take ownership of behaviors and actions. Implementing the Playbook for the team helped, but empowerment & transparency are also critical components to taking ownership. There are many ways for a leader to see when the tide begins to turn:

- Team members make comments about wanting to be a part of the solution.

- Team members take initiative to accomplish a task before a leader provides direction.

- Team members come to the leader about a mistake that was made that he/she intended to adjust (knowing he/she will not be reprimanded for the mistake).

- During a team audit, the team members ask the leader how the team is doing against the audit.

I had my Asset Protection senior leader come to me after the team just passed the Food & Safety Audit that occurred once a year. This was the third year of the audit in our journey to develop a high-performing team, and the whole team was prepared for the auditor to come into the building at any point. There was an SOP on how to react to an audit or disruption in the operation. Each leader in the building had tasks to complete in order to make sure the audit went well without impacting our customers by delaying the operation. Each leader had team members at all levels who had assignments as well. There were alternate team members in the event an assigned team member was absent during the audit. I randomly pretended to be an auditor throughout the year to check reaction times and provide real feedback. This particular audit went really well, and the senior AP leader came to me, very excited, and said, "Patrick, I had Bob (not real name) ask me how the audit was going and what he could do to help the team pass it. We want to pass this because we do not want to disappoint or fail the team." The team members were engaged and empowered to make decisions during the audit. After the audit, the leaders communicated to all the team members, with transparency, the successes and failures of the audit and the actions the team would take to correct it.

One hundred percent ownership at all levels is the ultimate goal for a leader of a team. Although you will never achieve perfection, you will, without a doubt, have a high-performing team of the highest caliber. This will be the end state of your journey. I must warn you: when your team is performing well and taking 100% ownership, you as the leader just worked yourself out of a job. The journey is long, hard, and takes persistence, but once it all comes together, your job is to see the icebergs ahead. You spend less time driving the business because there are others now doing that; things slow down, and your priority shifts to growing the culture of the team.

You could take this extra time and get complacent, taking a backseat, or you can dive into teaching your team more than you have before. Personally, I think teaching as much as you can to your teammates is a great use of your time and the most fulfilling responsibility of a leader. As you teach, you are investing in the future development of others.

KEY TAKEAWAYS OF CHAPTER 9:

1. The aim of 100% ownership is to build a lasting culture. It is not about delivering short-term business results.

2. Lead from the front as you show your team what taking 100% ownership looks like. If you model the way, your team members will emulate it.

3. Use See It, Own It, Fix It as a way to maintain the standard, emphasize structure, and promote 100% ownership at all levels.

4. A technique to model the way is having your team evaluate you with constructive feedback designed to help you become a better leader.

5. Empowering all team members and providing transparent information provides opportunities for all members to take ownership of their actions and behaviors.

CHAPTER TEN:

LEARNING FROM FAILURE

"Success is not final, failure is not fatal; it is the courage to continue that counts."

~ Winston Churchill

AS MUCH AS I would love to say that this book and process came about because I had two successful decades of leadership teaching, but the truth is that I failed a lot during my life thus far. However, my failures are what allowed me to figure out this process of building a championship team. And even when I thought I had the perfect Playbook to create a high-performance team, I sometimes neglected critical steps within the process. I want you to know that when you travel through this journey of building a team, no two teams are the same, and no two teams can be built the same way. You have to adjust and learn, but if you focus on the fundamentals of this book, it will steer you in the right direction. I want to make sure I point out some of my failures; one, because I take 100% ownership of them, and two, because I think they are important for you to be made aware of so you can avoid them. I am only talking about a few failures here, but believe me when I say there were many more.

FAILURE: TRUST & CREDIBILITY

The first failure I think is relevant actually occurred after I left the company, and the Eagles had completely turned around into a high-performing team. I truly believed I had figured out how to turn any size team around. I felt so strongly, I wrote a book about it. I left the company to join the manufacturing industry. I joined a smaller company near where I grew up; I was attracted by the smaller size, significant increase in salary, proximity to my family, promise of a quick promotion to a position of higher responsibility, and their desire for me to use my skill set to turn their manufacturing plant around. I remember the hiring director asking me if I was concerned about the complexity of a manufacturing plant versus a distribution center operation. My response was, "No, to me, the type of operation or business does not matter. Building a team is about leadership. It does not matter if it is a manufacturing environment, marketing team, sales team, finance team; leadership is about influencing a group of people in a positive way. It is about building trust and credibility, setting a vision, adding structure and organization, and instilling a culture of 100% ownership at all levels of the team." When I joined this team, it lacked structure, accountability, clarity, and leadership. I committed myself to using the Playbook I developed thus far in my career to change the culture.

I made a huge mistake by thinking I could pick up where I left off at my previous company with this new company. I believed that my reputation and explaining how the leaders and I changed the culture at my previous company would immediately give me enough credibility at this new company to move faster than the team was ready for. I knew in my heart this new team lacked structure, accountability, and ownership at all levels of the manufacturing plant. Everyone was out for themselves, and no one focused on the results of the team. There were several managers who were fighting fires in a similar manner to what I saw at my distribution center in the beginning days of forming the Eagles. I went right to work implementing structure by developing Standard Operating Procedures, teaching about leadership, and examining the inefficiencies.

A portion of my leadership team bought into the process, but some managers were just not going to support me because they could not get to the necessary mindset required for positive change. If you remember from Chapter 2, I explained that trust and credibility are the foundation of leadership, and that they are two of the first things that must be established before a leader does anything else. I failed to take the necessary time to build trust with my leaders, peers, and teammates. Because I failed to build trust with this new team, I also lacked credibility. As a result, any movement toward making the team better was met with significant resistance behind my back. Because I was an outsider in their eyes, I needed to be removed. I believed I had the foresight to see through the fog and guide the team to success. I believed I could see the end states because of my experiences.

I might well have known how to make the team successful, but I never got the chance because I failed to bring the team along with me. After five months in the company, my team was making progress and the major problems with backorders had significantly improved, but the leadership team soon let me know I was not a good fit for their culture. Every time–and I do mean EVERY time–you take over a new team, you MUST start from scratch. You must start the process over with building trust and credibility. I learned so much about myself from my manufacturing company failure that I do not have any ill will toward the company. I would not be where I am today to teach you about this failure without my five-month stint there. I hate that I failed the leaders and teammates with whom I did build a connection and who believed in my approach while I was there, but at least I have a lesson to learn from and now, so do you!

Failure: Do not build a team around yourself

Another pertinent failure worth mentioning occurred after I had just left the Army and joined my first corporation as an Operations Manager. I did not know anything about distribution center operations. Heck! I did not know much about business in general. I had been wearing a uniform for the past 12 years, talking military jargon, and flying helicopters, so I had to focus all of my time and effort on learning the business. I spent hours getting to know the hourly team members and leaders. I asked a lot of questions. I did not pretend to be smart about how to run a distribution operation. As time passed, I began to understand the operation more and started taking steps toward rebuilding the team around the picture I had of what a team should be. I truly believed the team should rely on standards and discipline. I thought we needed a team identity to help bring us all together. I took all the steps outlined in this book about building trust and credibility, setting goals for the team, influencing my teammates to be better each day and to think about the business differently than they had in the past.

Within seven months, I gained a lot of traction. The results started to show in safety, performance, and engagement. Turnover declined and team members gained more experience. We were no longer the laughingstock of the company. I built the whole team around ME. I was the driver of the team and the person who determined the success or failure. I was the motivator, decision maker, and key element to making everything work. In my heart, I kept telling myself, "Ok, we are clicking with my plan. Now, I need to figure out a way to transfer ownership because the mark of a good leader is how successful the team is even when they are not present." Because of the quick success, the senior leadership team took me from the team and asked me to go lead another team in another building.

I will never forget bringing in all 100 of my team members and leaders to explain to them that I would be leaving, but that this team was in good hands. The faces of several of the hourly team members–those who had truly bought into my vision for the team–looked like a deer in headlights. It was clear they felt blindsided and disappointed. One team member walked out and said, "Welp, he is gone. That's it. We are done as a team." I tried to explain that everything would be okay, that they could continue the progress without me. Because of the nature of my move to another team, this was the last day I saw those team members.

I spent the rest of the night walking the floor and shaking hands with everyone to thank them for their hard work and dedication to the team. It was emotional because I had developed a connection with each of them. I knew their families, interests, birthdays, and truly cared about their well-being. I was used to moving from team to team from my time in the Army, but it was still difficult.

I started on my new team a few days later and dove into starting the process of building a team all over again. One month later, I was contacted by one of my leaders from my previous team. He informed me that 80% of the hourly team members had either left the team for another one within the company or left the company altogether. Two of the four leaders left as well. The team was in last place (performance) and already had three injuries when they had not had an injury in over a year. I asked, "What happened?" My former leader explained, "After you left, everyone went back to the old ways of doing things. The new manager did not hold anyone accountable and stayed in his office all night. The team felt abandoned and lost purpose and interest in the job."

This was a serious blow! It was clear that I had failed my team. I was completely focused on results and doing things my way because I thought I knew what was best for the whole team. Because of this mindset, the team was clearly built around me. There was no empowerment or ownership instilled into the team. They relied on my leadership. I did not develop my leaders enough to take the reins and keep the culture strong. When I was leading the team, it seemed like I was empowering others and developing my leaders. It seemed like I was teaching others the "why" behind the vision and direction. It seemed like I was out in front of the team influencing them to follow me. But now I see that, in reality, I was behind them pushing them toward success.

Because the whole team and vision was built around me, that led to the disintegration of this particular team after I left. I immediately changed my approach with the new team and began to think of ways to ensure that the team would be built around the team members and leaders in the building instead of me. This lesson stuck with me throughout my career. Being the leader of a team is temporary, but the influence can be lasting if the core of the team is empowered and takes 100% ownership of the success of the team. Again, this mindset works in many different fields to include marketing, finance, procurement, sales, and operations. If you are a leader of or within a team, think about the lasting impact after you move onto your next position. Think about the legacy in which you will leave to the team.

FAILURE: BE CAREFUL HOW YOU EMAIL THE TEAM

As a reader, you have most likely picked up that I am a leader who believes in a standard and wants the team to meet or exceed that standard. Hopefully, you've also gathered that I want to win the right way, and that I will not tolerate poor standards or discipline. I do not like Nick Saban on principle because I am a die-hard Notre Dame fan, but I am an advocate of his leadership style. Saban believes in a process and having the discipline to play four quarters of a football game doing the little things right for every play. He has said that mediocre people do not like high performers and high performers do not like mediocre people. Everyone on the team has to buy into the same high standards.[1] As a result, you will see Saban on the sideline with three minutes left in the football game with his team up by 50 points disciplining a player who did not perform to standard. He doesn't care if the player is first or third string, the standard remains the same.

This is similar to the mindset that I took with the Eagles leaders. The team built great momentum and had the structure in place to be successful, but a few mediocre individuals who refused to buy into the team vision continued to be the "Ed Harris character" (from the National Treasure: Book of Secrets referenced earlier in the book), knocking the team out of balance. As a result, I spent time walking the floor only to see things that were obviously not within the standards we had set forth as a team. My emotions got the better of me on many of those walks. To be fair to the team, there were more areas of the business held to the standard than not, but the opportunities I saw were the little things that I knew would become bigger, and that would impact the future progress of the team. I wrote many notes, and took pictures to be able to show examples of these missed opportunity areas. After walking the operational floor for a few hours, I sat down at my desk to communicate to the leaders through email, as if each one was in the office with me. I wrote direct comments to individuals, expressed my disappointment in the missed opportunities, and voiced my frustration around not performing the little tasks to standard. I sometimes used sarcasm in the email that sounded fine in my head, but words on a screen or on paper are interpreted differently by every individual. It is why communicating clear directions in an email or text is extremely difficult. It is also ill advised. My intention behind the emails was to make the team better because I truly cared about the vision and what it took to make the progress necessary to achieve the goals the team set forth, but that's not how the emails came across to those receiving them. As my leaders told me, these emails were ineffective with the team members and did more harm than good. They were like "angry tweets" as one leader so "eloquent-ly" put it. I then spent so much time explaining the intent and meaning behind some of the emails that the message I was trying to convey ended up getting lost.

What I learned is that email can be an effective communication tool, but should be utilized to provide general information, not as an accountability tool. My approach to emails was lazy leadership, which created barriers between my leaders and me. In addition, every time I pressed "send" on one of these emails, I lost credibility with the team and the point was lost. A more effective approach would be to grab a leader and a few other team members to walk with me and first point out the positive things I saw followed by the areas needing improvement. There is a greater impact when talking face to face about the trickle-down effects if the improvement/opportunity areas continue to be ignored. To build trust, I should have put the ownership on the leader to communicate to the rest of the leaders on different shifts. Then, I could have discussed what I saw in one-on-one conversations with the leaders. This takes more time and effort than an "email blast," but builds trust versus losing credibility. It also builds a healthy relationship.

Because my leaders felt comfortable telling me about the impact of the emails, I adjusted my approach and instituted a weekly walk on each shift with an hourly team member and their direct leader. Together, we walked the operational floor looking at the standards and disciplines of the team. It was engaging and a two-way conversation where the team member asked questions of me and I of him/her about the vision and goals of the building and what we were trying to achieve as an overall team. After the walk, we discussed what actions the leader and hourly team member could take to ensure proper communication flow to the rest of the team. They owned the actions needed to improve on the areas of opportunity, and continue doing the things that move the team toward the vision. At times, I emailed the whole team as a follow up to one of the walks to help carry the message, but not in an "angry tweet" format.

LESSON LEARNED: CHOICES MADE

Leaders reading this book must understand that I was still learning while doing this and, as a result, I failed many times. However, I learned from the mistakes I made. I want to make sure I call myself out on these lessons learned in order to help prevent you from falling into some of these traps. But, rest assured, you will still make mistakes; you will let your team down; you will let yourself down; and you will feel alone at times; but you will prevail if you trust that failure is part of the process of getting better and striving for excellence. Building a team takes a lot of work. There are long days and never enough hours to accomplish everything within the seemingly unreasonable deadlines the company often sets.

1. Where do you spend your initial time?
   - Do you spend it in your office looking at numbers? Do you spend it with the hourly team members on the floor? Or do you spend it with your leaders? It is difficult to put the necessary level of time into all three of these areas, and it is equally difficult to choose which is most important.

- Initially, I chose to spend my time with my leadership team. I invested a lot of time here in the beginning of developing the Eagles, which hurt me later on when momentum built because my leaders were not strong enough yet to have the right conversations with the team members on the floor. As a result, the letter was written that I discussed earlier in the book that derailed our progress. It was necessary to grow from that experience, but it nonetheless impacted the progress the team had made to that point. Ultimately, this was my responsibility and my fault because I did not explain more of the "why" to the team members on the ground floor executing the operation. It is important to try to find the balance when establishing trust and credibility.

2. Is it hard for you to be vulnerable?

- I struggled to be vulnerable in the beginning of building the Eagles. I wanted to seem like a "tough-guy leader." I wanted to be the "rock" for my team and, as a result, shut down emotionally to everyone. I was laser-focused on not building the team around myself because I knew I would not be there forever and had learned from mistakes with my first team at the initial distribution center. I did not let anyone inside my head because I knew I would have to make tough decisions along the way, and I did not want to let emotions get the best of me. This was something I developed over time while being in the Army and being deployed. I read many books and listened to leadership podcasts that argued that the best approach in leadership was to be caring with empathy and to be vulnerable, but I still neglected to exercise those teachings. As a result, many leaders and team members struggled to make a connection with me despite respecting my level of knowledge and best intentions for the team.

- I finally learned a lesson in vulnerability about 18 months into joining the team. I was getting my MBA at Notre Dame, and during my first week at school I participated in an exercise where I had to tell my personal story in front of 55 students who were strangers to me at the time. I was the first to speak in the class and while telling my story, I became emotional; however, I quickly realized it opened the door for the whole MBA class to be vulnerable. Our class had an instant connection that day. A month after that class, I decided to take down my emotional walls with my Eagles team and tell my story. I invited other leaders to share their stories as well. From that moment on, I was more open. I still did not talk much about the military or the deployments unless someone asked, but I began to develop personal connections with my leaders and team members from that point forward. The books and podcast were correct. As Brené Brown says, "Vulnerability is the birthplace of innovation, creativity, and change."[2] In order to move the team into the Performing Stage, I had to be vulnerable because it is also a big part of building trust.

3. You cannot do it alone:

- I tried to do all of it myself in the beginning of building the Eagles team. While I was working hard to build trust with team members, I still did not trust them to take the journey with me. I was confident of myself because all my life I had set goals and then did everything I could to ensure I accomplished them. As a result, as the teams got bigger and the tasks got tougher, it was impossible for me to do everything alone and do it the right way. I overextended myself and missed a lot of things I normally would catch. There was no one looking out for the iceberg ahead to prevent the team from running into unnecessary issues.

- Lean on your leaders who commit early to what you are trying to accomplish. I had a strong leader with a military background who understood immediately why the team had to take a different direction than it had in the past. After a year of me leading the team, she pulled me to the side and said, "Patrick, you do not have to do it all by yourself. Let the team help. There are enough of us far along in the journey where we can help guide the ship." She was right, and it felt like a weight had been lifted from me.

CLOSING: STAYING HUMBLE/OWNERSHIP STARTS WITH "WHY"

I am sure everyone has had that moment where they look back at their life and can make connection points as to why things happened the way they did. While going through the situation, there was most likely a plethora of emotions anywhere from joy, anger, sadness, or anxiety. It might have involved a birth, break-up, death of a family member, promotion, loss of a job, injury, or some other life-altering event. In difficult moments, it's hard not to think the world is out to get you; that God is out to get you. I can assure you; I look back at my life to this point and think about how I had the worst luck, but things always seemed to work out. Even when you believe everything will work out, it does not make it easier in the moment.

I started this book with the roots of my leadership to provide you, as the reader, some insight into the beginning of my journey and then ended with very direct and truthful learnings from my failures. Without the failures, I would not have grown to be the leader I am today. Hopefully, you picked up on some of the trials and tribulations I experienced throughout my career to this point, and I hope this gives you solace that no matter how challenging a situation becomes, you will come out on the other end better than when you started. You do not have to be a CEO, General in the Army, or high level Executive to make a positive impact on your team and company. Never let hard and challenging times pass you by without experiencing personal growth and capturing those lessons learned that you can use in the future to better yourself or others.

If this book inspired you,
please pass it along to someone you want to inspire.

AFTERWORD

WHEN I LOOK BACK on my time with the Eagles, the thing I am most proud of is the success of many of my teammates. Many of the hourly team members are now mid-level and senior leaders within the company. Many have connected with me via LinkedIn and phone to check in and provide updates. Three of my senior leaders are now leading their own distribution centers and have mentioned that they brought with them several tools from our journey together. Other teammates left the company for a promotion to work for other supply chain companies. They are successful and teach others the fundamentals of team building. Every now and then a leader will reach out to me to talk about our transformational journey. It is always fun to reminisce about the challenges endured, successes achieved, and fun moments shared.

After spending about 13 years in operations leading different teams of all sizes, I decided to disrupt myself and transition careers. It took my wife and I five years to have our first child. Throughout our infertility journey, we tried everything possible leading up to in vitro fertilization (IVF). It was a long, stressful process. Throughout the long journey I gained a perspective on what I wanted for my life. While working in Florida, we had our first child and the operational work-life balance was not ideal. Turning around a low-performing team takes a lot of time and effort. I wanted to spend as much time as possible with my children. I was good at my job, but I was also working 24/7 because I had four different shifts, so I was "always on" even if I was not inside the distribution center. My company asked me to go fix another team in another part of the country, and this was not something I wanted for my life at this stage with a young family.

I never imagined transitioning careers would be so difficult. I could write another book on the process of the transition from one career field to another. I leveraged an M.B.A from the University of Notre Dame Mendoza College of Business to help. I spent two years earning my degree and networking with amazing people from my program. I reached out to my West Point network to help me get started on figuring out what I wanted to do that would satisfy my need for a better life-work balance not in operations. I explored careers in private equity, consulting, executive recruiting, executive coaching, procurement, and human resources. I engaged with so many great people—some complete strangers—willing to help and point me in the right direction. I truly looked forward to every conversation because I never knew where it might lead. For example, I reached out to a West Pointer for advice on executive recruiting, and he linked me up with three other great people to talk to. This happened over and over again.

I documented every conversation I had with these individuals in my network, and eventually met a business leader who gave me some great advice. He said, "Patrick, you need to understand something. You have an amazing background and I know you could do anything you set your mind to, but all the risk is on me. All the risk is on the hiring company. All of your experience is in operations, so you will not be able to transition careers at the same level as you currently are." This made it real; if I was to transition careers and truly disrupt myself, I would have to take one, maybe three steps back in my career. I knew in my heart this was still the right path, and this advice enabled me to get laser-focused on figuring out what I wanted to do next.

I came across a company with great leaders willing to take a chance on me. I found a marketing role that combined the brand and product sides of the business. I lacked brand marketing experience, and the little exposure I had came from my M.B.A. program. I did not have product marketing experience in the traditional sense, but product marketing has a lot of similarities to what I experienced over the previous 13 years in the Army and operations. I believed I could leverage my past experience to do well on the product marketing side of the role, and use my learning agility and people around me to learn the brand marketing side. During the interview process, I showed how my background thus far in my career could lend itself well to this new career path, and the leaders agreed I could think differently and elevate the business in a positive way.

I went from leading 900 team members to zero when I transitioned careers to marketing. This caught me off guard and bothered me more than I thought because I love leadership and the positive influence I can have on other people. But, when I joined the new company, I went back to my roots and said to myself, "it's time to build trust and credibility with the new team." That is exactly what I did. I began meeting with every cross-functional partner within the scope of the role. I used everything I wrote about in this book to help my leaders, who had taken a chance on me, to build a high-performance team. As I grew with this marketing team and company, we posted record sales four years in a row, launched many new products into the market, established a new brand, redefined the brand fundamentals of an existing brand, and created a culture others within the company wanted to be a part of.

No matter the size of a team, the career field, or the rank you hold within a team, the principles and process remain the same.

ACKNOWLEDGMENTS

THIS IS THE FIRST BOOK I have written, and it has given me respect for the many authors who write books for a living. It is not easy to keep the whole story together over the long period of time it takes to write it. I hope I did a good job of acknowledging the work and impact these great authors and leaders had on my life. This book took me over three years to write once I committed to telling the story. Several individual teammates throughout my career said I should write a book about my leadership approach to team building. I did not think I could find the time with a growing family, but those were just excuses I gave myself for not doing it. Without those individuals, I would not have thought I had anything of substance that people would want to read because I did not have the high rank, title, or "career experience."

There is no doubt I am still learning and growing as a husband, father, friend, and leader, but I believe in this process. I continue to make mistakes and learn from them in order to improve. My wife, Katherine, is someone who continues to push me to do better. She is my beacon to keep me on the straight and narrow. Her continual encouragement to document my life for our children has been a great inspiration. To our children, Grace, Wyatt, and Caroline, I hope this gives you a glimpse of what a portion of my life was like. Thank you to all my teammates who trusted me to lead. Thank you to the reader for taking the invitation, and for your investment in my story.

APPENDIX

LEADERSHIP CONTRACT

TO: Eagles Leadership Team

SUBJECT: A Pledge for as long as I am a Leader

I pledge to the Leadership Team:

1. To set the right example by my own actions in all things.
2. To be consistent in my temperament so that the team knows how to "read" me and what to expect from me.
3. To be fair, impartial, and consistent in matters relating to work rules, discipline, and rewards.
4. To show a sincere, personal interest in team members as individuals without becoming overly familiar.
5. To seek team counsel on matters that affect their jobs and to be guided as much as possible by their judgment.
6. To allow team members as much individuality as possible in the way their jobs are performed, as long as the quality of the end result is not compromised.
7. To make sure the team always knows in advance what I expect from them in the way of conduct and performance on the job.
8. To be appreciative of team efforts and generous in praise of their accomplishments.
9. To use every opportunity to teach team members how to do their jobs better and how to help themselves advance in skill level and responsibility.
10. To show the team that I can "do" as well as "lead" by pitching in to work beside team members when my help is needed.

"A leader is a rare person who comes along, raises the standards of excellence, and inspires a group of individuals to achieve the impossible"

Patrick Hall   Leader

FLOW OF ANNUAL EVALUATIONS
1. Formality:
   a. Introduction / How did the year go in their minds?
   b. Initial counseling:
   c. Recap of the year:
      i. Vision/goal-setting, Part Two
      ii. Safety even from previous year
      iii. 17 new leaders added to team
      iv. TY: 177.48 vs. LY: 168.97 (5.04% increase & 8.88% increase in two years)
      v. $.90 associate incentive for three quarters
      vi. All audits passed
      vii. CPCS maxed out for the year
      viii. Hurricanes, capacity issues, battery power inefficiencies
      ix. 15-year celebration and several other cookouts
   d. Evaluation rating
   e. Go over evaluation briefly and give the leader three minutes to read over it.
2. Performance metrics sheet
   a. Walk through the Excel sheet printout
   b. Performance notes
3. Sustains/improves:
4. Expectations:
   a. Turnover: This is costing us three to five UPH a day
   b. Safety: Poor behaviors. More lucky than proactive
   c. Building CPH: 194
   d. Quality: Gross adjustments will change and improve
   e. Customer service: LSI responses & VCOE
   f. Finish a full year from start to finish
   g. Volume does not dictate what the performance or disciplines are in the building

    h. Challenge the process and status quo. Challenge your leaders

    i. Be more prepared for meetings and more active with ideas. Own the message

    j. Make this team YOUR team

5.   Financial sheet review

6.   Closing

LEADERS GUIDANCE SHEET

Week 25

1. Standards & Disciplines:
    a. Dry side team- Focus on it
    b. Emphasize to wrapper team members to use cleaning bags.
2. Performance: We need to project above goal to have a chance
3. Retention: Inform your team members about the plan for the week
   Team Member Meeting: Ensure your associates show up on time and are informed
4. Haulers: All hauler performance sent by end of workweek
5. Hydrogen Batteries: End of shift Parking Program is critical now more than ever. Before team members leave for the day, they will en sure that the batteries are 100% full of hydrogen.
6. Shareholder Names to HR: Communicate to associates and get names to HR
7. 15-Year Lanyards: Hand out to our team members.
8. Game Plan for Success Updates:
    a. Battle of the Bands General Meeting: Saturday
    b. Operation Mother's Day
    c. All leader meeting preparation
    d. Memorial Day preparation
    e. Leadercast Reminder: Enter date
9. Meetings:
    a. Case per man-hour analysis meeting: Daily at 2:30
    b. Eagle Elite Program: Monday & Tuesday. Last Class is on

---

10. Have Fun:

"Your attitude, not your aptitude, will determine your altitude."

~Zig Ziglar

ENDNOTES

Introduction:

1. Neves, Antonio. 2018. "It's 2018 and People Still Hate Millennials. Here Are 4 Reasons Why." Inc.com. Inc. March 7, 2018. https://www.inc.com/antonio-neves/the-real-reason-that-older-generations-hate-millennials-is-not-what-you-think.html.

Chapter 1:

1. Wikipedia Contributors. 2020. "World Trade Center (2001–Present)." Wikipedia. Wikimedia Foundation. October 28, 2020.https://en.wikipedia.org/wiki/World_Trade_Center_(2001%E2%80%93present).
2. Information on the construction One World Trade Center Tower and 9/11 Memorial Museum: Wikipedia Contributors. 2020. "World Trade Center (2001–Present)." Wikipedia. Wikimedia Foundation. October 28, 2020. https://en.wikipedia.org/wiki/World_Trade_Center_(2001%E2%80%93present).
3. Doran, George. 1981. Review of There's a S.M.A.R.T. Way to Write Management Goals and Objectives.

Chapter 2:

1. Tuckman, Bruce W. 1965. "Developmental Sequence in Small Groups." Psychological Bulletin 63 (6): 384–99.
2. Ramsey, Dave. 2012. Entreleadership: 20 Years of Practical Business Wisdom from the Trenches. Howard Books. This is where I learned the phrase, "excellent in the ordinary".
3. "Leadercast 2016: Architects of Tomorrow // Andy Stanley." n.d. www.youtube.com.https://www.youtube.com/watch?v=zAOg_rGVlr4.
4. Collins, Jim. 2001. Good to Great: Why Some Companies Make the Leap ... And Others Don't. London: Random House.
5. Albert Einstein quoted, "No problem can be solved from the same level of consciousness that created it. You have to rise above it."

Chapter 3:

1. Kouzes, James M, and Barry Z Posner. 2017. The Leadership Challenge. San Francisco, Calif. Jossey-Bass.

2. "Definition of TRUST." 2019. Merriam-Webster.com. 2019. https://www.merriam-webster.com/dictionary/trust.

3. Webster, Merriam. 2019. "Definition of CREDIBILITY." Merriam-Webster.com. 2019. https://www.merriam-webster.com/dictionary/credibility.

4. Keating, Steve. 2017. Review of Invest in Trust. August 10, 2017. https://stevekeating.me/tag/credibility-bank/.

5. Keating, Steve. 2017. Review of Invest in Trust. August 10, 2017. https://stevekeating.me/tag/credibility-bank/.

6. Brown, Brene. 2018. Dare to Lead: Brave Work. Tough Conversations. Whole Hearts. New York: Random House.

7. Ramsey, Dave. 2012. Entreleadership: 20 Years of Practical Business Wisdom from the Trenches. Howard Books.

Chapter 4:

1. "Prepped the battlefield" is a term used in the army as a tactic to soften the enemy in preparation for an engagement. I used this term in the book as a way to explain my approach to getting ready to teach my team about vision setting.

2. Ray, Stephanie. 2021. Review of What Is a Vision Statement? 15 Vision Statement Examples to Inspire You. November 12, 2021. https://www.projectmanager.com/blog/guide-writing-perfect-vision-statement-examples.

3. Sinek, Simon. 2009. Start with Why: How Great Leaders Inspire Everyone to Take Action. London: Portfolio/Penguin.

4. Blanchard, Ken. 2019. WHALE DONE! : The Power of Positive Relationships.

Chapter 5:

1. Cristol, Hope. 2019. "What Is Dopamine?" WebMD. WebMD. June 19, 2019. https://www.webmd.com/mental-health/what-is-dopamine#1.

2. Julson, Erica. 2018. "10 Best Ways to Increase Dopamine Levels Naturally." Healthline. Healthline Media. May 10, 2018. https://www.healthline.com/nutrition/how-to-increase-dopamine.

3. Michael Jordan quote

4. Kenton, Will. 2021. "Organizational Structure." Investopedia. November 10, 2021. https://www.investopedia.com/terms/o/organizational-structure.asp.

5. Tuckman, Bruce W. 1965. "Developmental Sequence in Small Groups." Psychological Bulletin 63 (6): 384–99.

6. Wolff, Florence I, and Nadine C Marsnik. 1992. Perceptive Listening. Fort Worth Tex.: Harcourt Brace Jovanovich College Publishers.

7. Brown, Brene. 2018. Dare to Lead: Brave Work. Tough Conversations. Whole Hearts. New York: Random House.

8. Blanchard, Ken. 2019. WHALE DONE!: The Power of Positive Relationships.

9. Wooden, John R, Steve Jamison, and Inc Ebrary. 2005. Wooden on Leadership. New York: Mcgraw-Hill.

10. Bigman, Dan. 2020. "Lencioni: Why Do You Want to Be a CEO?" ChiefExecutive.net. April 23, 2020. https://chiefexecutive.net/lencioni-why-do-you-want-to-be-a-ceo/. In listening to Podcasts with Patrick Lencioni & Dave Ramsey, I heard both of them refer to the CEO as the Chief Execution Officer, which made an impact on me and I used that term while teaching and building my team.

11. Heath, Chip, and Dan Heath. 2013. Switch: How to Change Things When Change Is Hard. Erscheinungsort Nicht Ermittelbar: Random House Us.

12. Maxwell, John C. 2007. The 21 Irrefutable Laws of Leadership. Nashville: Thomas Nelson.

13. Ramsey, Dave. 2012. Entreleadership: 20 Years of Practical Business Wisdom from the Trenches. Howard Books.

Chapter 6:
1. Willink, Jocko, and Leif Babin. 2018. Extreme Ownership: How U.S. Navy SEALs Lead and Win. Sydney, N.S.W.: Macmillan.
2. Berry, Tim. 2015. "Business Strategy Is Useless without Execution." Tim Berry. March 4, 2015. https://timberry.com/strategy-is-use-less-without-execution/#:~:text=To%20my%20mind%2C%20strat-egy%20without. I took elements from Tim Berry's quote, "Good business planning is 9 parts execution for every 1 part strategy" to come up with the phrase, "One point for planning and nine points for execution". I believed it was applicable to what I was teaching my team.
3. Levine, Michael. 2021. Broken Windows, Broken Business: The Revolutionary Broken Windows Theory: How the Smallest Remedies Reap the Biggest Rewards. New York: Grand Central Publishing.

Chapter 7:
1. "Episode 74 - Train to Retain." n.d. Leadership Today. https://leadership.today/episodes/2020/4/18/episode-74-train-to-retain.
2. Liker, Jeffrey K, and Gary L Convis. 2012. The Toyota Way to Lean Leadership: Achieving and Sustaining Excellence through Leadership Development. Maidenhead: Mcgraw-Hill Professional.
3. Liker, Jeffrey K, and Gary L Convis. 2012. The Toyota Way to Lean Leadership: Achieving and Sustaining Excellence through Leadership Development. Maidenhead: Mcgraw-Hill Professional.
4. Williams, Pat, and Jim Denney. 2018. Leadership Excellence. Charleston, South Carolina: Advantage.
5. Holmes, Andy. n.d. "3 Great Mentoring Relationships throughout History." www.mentorresources.com. https://www.mentorresourc-

es.com/mentoring-blog/3-great-mentoring-relationships-through-out-history.

6. Lencioni, Patrick. 2016. The Ideal Team Player: How to Recognize and Cultivate the Three Essential Virtues: A Leadership Fable. Hoboken, Nj Jossey-Bass.

7. Lencioni, Patrick. 2016. The Ideal Team Player: How to Recognize and Cultivate the Three Essential Virtues: A Leadership Fable. Hoboken, Nj Jossey-Bass.

8. Lencioni, Patrick. 2016. The Ideal Team Player: How to Recognize and Cultivate the Three Essential Virtues: A Leadership Fable. Hoboken, Nj Jossey-Bass.

Chapter 8:

1. Albert Einstein quoted, "No problem can be solved from the same level of consciousness that created it. You have to rise above it."

2. "Wojciechowski: Starr Remembers Lombardi's Impact." 2006. ESPN.com. February 3, 2006. https://www.espn.com/espn/columns/story?columnist=wojciechowski_gene&id=2318158.

3. Ramsey, Dave. 2012. Entreleadership: 20 Years of Practical Business Wisdom from the Trenches. Howard Books.

4. "Leadercast 2014: Beyond You // Andy Stanley." n.d. www.youtube.com. https://www.youtube.com/watch?v=8ru6oYxeqas.

5. Johnson, Whitney. 2015. Disrupt Yourself: Putting the Power of Disruptive Innovation to Work. Brookline, Ma: Bibliomotion.

6. Wikipedia Contributors. 2019. "Learning Curve." Wikipedia. Wikimedia Foundation. June 25, 2019. https://en.wikipedia.org/wiki/Learning_curve.

7. Joel Arthur Barker. 1994. Paradigms: The Business of Discovering the Future. Melbourne: Information Australia.

8. I spoke to four of my leaders from the company, and I compiled what they said and put it into the book.

9. Liker, Jeffrey K, and Gary L Convis. 2012. The Toyota Way to Lean Leadership: Achieving and Sustaining Excellence through Lead-

ership Development. Maidenhead: Mcgraw-Hill Professional. I learned about the phrase in a class, which came from this book.

Chapter 9:
1. Sinek, Simon. 2020. Infinite Game. S.L.: Portfolio Penguin.
2. Connors, Roger, Tom Smith, and Craig R Hickman. 2010. The Oz Principle: Getting Results through Individual and Organizational Accountability. New York: Portfolio.
3. Jesse And Russell. 2012. Broken Windows Theory. Edinburgh, Scotland: Lennex Corp. The theory was first introduced in an article by James Q Wilson and George L. Kelling in 1982.

Chapter 10:
1. "Nick Saban's Mediocre Speech." n.d. Vimeo.com. https://vimeo.com/530785835.
2. Brené Brown. 2010. "The Power of Vulnerability." Ted.com. TED Talks. June 2010. https://www.ted.com/talks/brene_brown_the_power_of_vulnerability?language=en.